Eléonore Bille-De Mot · THE AGE OF AKHENATEN

Eléonore Bille-De Mot

# THE AGE OF AKHENATEN

McGRAW-HILL BOOK COMPANY

New York · Toronto

WINGATE COLLEGE LIBRARY
WINGATE, N. C.

Translated from the French by Jack Lindsay

© 1966 Cory, Adams & Mackay Ltd.
All rights reserved
Library of Congress Catalogue Card Number 66–22349
05268

Printed in Great Britain

# CONTENTS

35575

# PREFACE

On the first page of my book I want to inscribe the name of Jean Capart, who was friend and colleague of my father. They worked side by side in related disciplines; together they visited Egypt and Greece and took part in many archaeological congresses. When then I was received for the first time by the Director of the Egyptian Section in the Musée du Cinquantenaire at Brussels, it was not as a mere student but to some extent as a daughter who for more than a quarter of a century had claimed every attention and indulgence. The Egyptologist perhaps divined, beneath the first signs of a sense of vocation, a profound desire for self-identification with a lost and regretted father.

I am happy today to be able to express my gratitude to him who was my Master, by dedicating this work to his memory.

My sincere thanks go also, first of all, to Mr Norbert Schimmel of New York, who has allowed me to publish the admirable reliefs from his collection, as well as to Mr John D. Cooney of the Cleveland Museum, who has kindly supplied me with all information concerning these reliefs; then to the directors of various museums who have given me permission to make colour-reproductions of objects in their charge.

Further, I should like to thank my colleagues and friends of long standing in the Fondation Égyptologique Reine Elizabeth, Pierre Gilbert, Director, and Arpag Mekhitarian, General Secretary, who have allowed me to draw on the Fondation's photographic archives. An experienced photographer, M. Mekhitarian, has greatly eased my work in the choice and the impression of photographic proofs.

To all, I express my gratitude for the help they have so generously given me.

Brussels, 1965

# INTRODUCTION

To present a coherent account of the events that took place in Amarna during the decade and a half when it was the capital of Egypt is a difficult undertaking. In spite of the numerous surviving documents, significant historical data scarcely exist. We possess an abundance of evidence warranting a reconstruction of the material civilization, but a paucity of definite dates for determining the sequence of incidents as they came about in the course of this period. Contemporary archives, such as the diplomatic correspondence found on the spot, provide few chronological signposts. Even if they reflect in a remarkably vivid way the situation beyond the Egyptian frontiers, they make it appear peculiarly entangled. Since the discovery of Tutankhamen's tomb at Thebes in 1923, and the systematic excavation of the Amarna site, eminent Egyptologists have striven to establish the historical framework of a period which the ancient Egyptians themselves had taken every care to wipe out of man's memory. The suggestions of scholars, sometimes contradictory, have not cleared up in a way at all satisfactory the problems of what one of them calls this 'exasperating period'.[1] While adopting the hypotheses which we consider sound, we have in turn attempted to set out our own point of view; and to avoid wearying the non-specialist reader, we have consigned to notes the arguments which seem to support our conjectures. Matters which may seem irrefutable today are always at the mercy of new discoveries; we shall therefore regard the conjectures as working hypotheses, with the hope that some day they will be confirmed.

'True history', wrote the late Réné Grousset, 'is not that of the ebb and flow of frontiers. It is that of civilization. And civilization is on one hand the progress of techniques, on the other hand it is spiritual progress.'[2] Among techniques, the plastic arts have always held a choice place in archaic societies. Not the place that we assign to them today; for, belonging to the sphere of the crafts, they were then dominated by religion and magic. And this was true to such an extent that the Egyptian has been described almost as a 'fetish-maker'.[3] Few names of artists have come down to us. Authors did not sign their work, which remained normally anonymous. This evident *impersonality* of Pharaonic art has inclined certain Egyptologists to deny it any creative individuality.[4] Though this position may seem firmly based, we cannot unreservedly accept it for the great epochs. The creator of the fine Chephren in diorite, the portraitist who carved the face of Prince Ankh-haf, the one who cut out of dark granite the disillusioned features of Sesostris III, finally the head-sculptor Tuthmosis who at Amarna sculptured the effigies of Akhenaten and his family, were all artists in the noblest sense of the term. They are entitled to rank among the greatest. Their contemporaries, besides, did not fail to admire them if we are to credit certain expressions: 'Lord of the Hand' and 'He who grasps reality forcefully by means of appearances that strike the eyes'.[5]

In the fourteenth century B.C. we behold one of the moments of intense creative activity, as Egypt entered into sustained contact with nations that are her equals in their degree of civilization. Peaceful penetration replaced earlier invasions; there is a short-lived and brilliant truce during which civilization reaches a new peak. We witness what was perhaps for the first time a genuine West-East meeting—one that was prelude to the endless discoveries of Asia, to the ever-unsatisfied nostalgia for the unknown which was over the ages to drag the Greeks in the train of Alexander, the Franks to the con-quest of Jerusalem, Marco Polo along the Silk Route, the Hispanic navigators on the quest for the treasures of Golconda . . .

By mating the poetry of the Orient with the spirit of wisdom and discretion of ancient Egypt, Akhenaten was able to inspire the artists of his time with a renewed vision of reality. Their sculptures often surpass the particular style of their age and rise to the level of the great creations of human genius. The sovereign had set himself to impose on his subjects and even on foreign peoples an ideal of love and brotherhood. If he failed, it was because the world was not yet ready to receive his message. His successors implacably condemned him; they effaced his name and wrecked his work. But we should like to think that among those who went with him on his enterprise without a future there were some who gave it a genuine enthusiasm.

Akhetaten, the lovely city of the heretical Pharaoh, is today a dead place. In spite of being deserted, the site has kept its beauty intact and remains as it was thirty centuries ago, when at every dawn Aten 'was resplendent on the horizon' for the greater happiness of its followers. Between the rose-coloured mountain and the riverbank where meagre crops grow green, the desert inexorably destroys the last traces of an evanescent dream. A few shacks of puddled clay rise up, scattered, in the midst of palm trees and fragile tamarisks. The metallic rustling of the palm leaves, the sharp grinding of a sakhieh, the bark of a dog, the braying of an ass or the harsh call of the hawk are the only sounds to disturb the profound quiet of the morning. The few travellers who, going up the Nile, make a brief halt there do not fail to be moved by the melancholy charm of the place. Stirred, they wander among the ruins and try to capture a last echo of the exalted faith which once animated certain spirits and allayed their thirst for the absolute.

Alongside historical incidences and material evidence with a severely limited set of references in time, the 'human phenomenon' remains constant across the centuries, even the millennia. A civilized man of more than three thousand years is as close to us as the *honnête homme* of Louis XIV's century. The XVIIIth dynasty of Egypt offers us enough proofs of its humanism to make us feel directly concerned, particularly through the Amarna interlude, a window opened on to a world that has passed away. Some of the customs of that time may appear odd to us; but the way in which Amarna sensibility revealed itself is quite comprehensible: its love of man and nature, its expression of regret, its religious ardour, its ideal of truth and justice come easily home to us. By putting ourselves inside the skin of the people, by bringing sympathy to bear on their sorrows and their joys, by daring at times to make use of a 'sort of imagination',[6] we believe that we do not distort the historical facts. By employing psychological traits to connect those facts together, we have sought to make the latter more attractive to the reader and to arouse in him a current of sympathy for the heroes of this tragic adventure.

# 1. EGYPT BEFORE THE SCHISM

When Homer sang of Egyptian Thebes 'where every dwelling is full of riches, the city of a hundred gates through each of which pass two hundred warriors with their horses and chariots . . .'[1] Thebes was already in decline and its glory was that of a great past. Only its enchanting reputation had survived.

We must go back to the time of the New Empire, in the fourteenth century B.C., to discover Egypt at the zenith of its power and its civilization. The great event of the XVIIIth dynasty, which had brought wealth and prosperity to the Nile Valley, was the conquest of a vast empire in Asia. This conquest was more than a revenge for the long humiliation caused by the Hyksos occupation; it was a necessary act to prevent the recurrence of foreign invasions, of which the last, a century and a half in duration, had destroyed the country's political unity.

After driving out the Hyksos (about 1580), the Theban dynasty, founded by Prince Ahmosis, had to take steps for definitely warding off a return offensive by the Palestinians or a large-scale irruption by the Nubians. They themselves attacked first, as previously, the Mentuhoteps and the Sesostrids had done. The policy of conquest thus went back to the Middle Empire, where it had been undertaken for the same reasons. But instead of being merely defensive as in the past, the military campaigns had become imperial. The Egyptian army no longer aimed at simply holding Gaza in the north or the second cataract in the south, the strategic limits of the XIIth dynasty. Now it had extended its area of control as far as the Euphrates on one side, and as far as the fifth cataract on the other, thus establishing the bases of an empire that reached simultaneously into both Asia and Africa.

The success of the war of independence, which had galvanized the dispersed forces of Egypt, was mainly due to a factor of much importance: improved armaments, which from now on raised operations to a new level, that of a war of movement. There is no proof that the Hyksos, at the time of their invasion, made use of horses, chariots, and iron weapons; but it is certain that these new arms had spread through the Valley of the Nile during the second half of their occupation. The policy of prestige, practised by the first kings of the XVIIIth dynasty, consolidated the victory which had driven out the

13

WINGATE COLLEGE LIBRARY
WINGATE, N. C.

Asians, by keeping them henceforth in their own lands, under Pharaonic rule. In crossing the threshold of the new territories and imposing its domination on them, the Egyptian empire became one of the chief factors in Oriental history; it carried on victoriously for almost five centuries.

The geographical position of the Nile Valley, isolated between its desert hills, and the wealth of its natural resources, had enabled Egypt, thanks to the authority of a strongly centralized State, to develop early a civilization with a highly specific character. Western Asia, on the contrary, offered great geographical variety, which involved an extensive ethnical diversity. In Syria and Mesopotamia the territory was cut up into city-states, distributed among populations of different races. As a result, its civilization had never owned the fundamental unity of Egyptian civilization; it functioned as the expression of varying groups and regions. Yet an essential common basis was always present, more or less apparent, more or less revealed in the art and architecture; and even if the tongues were diverse, cuneiform script became the international form of writing for political and commercial transactions.[2]

Necessities in the economic sphere, however, compelled Egypt from the very dawn of her history to come into contact with the outer world. Poor in mineral deposits, she had to take from Asia, from the fifth millennium onwards, the techniques of copper, and later those of bronze. Wood, the other indispensable material, came from the forests of Lebanon, whose lofty cedars provided ships' masts and beams for building. Coasting along, Egyptian ships sailed as far as Byblos, which had been from the earliest times the main exporting centre for Phoenician timber. In exchange Egypt brought the gold which she obtained from Nubia, her fine transparent linens, her faience, and even the small plain wares that were in time to be found plentifully in most of the towns of the Phoenician coast. The discovery of statues dedicated in the temples of Byblos, and even Qatna, testify to the importance of the Egyptian presence in Asia from the time of the Middle Kingdom, when Byblos already played the role of vassal. Possession of Syria and Palestine, which together formed a sort of natural corridor between the two continents, was of prime importance to the great powers, as much for strategic reasons as on account of the various trade routes meeting there.

The extremely mixed populations of these regions, Canaanites, Amorites, Hurrians, grouped under petty kings, around the ports and the strong towns of the interior. The sedentary folk were always more or less under the threat of the nomadic bands who infested the wooded mountains and desert borders. Yet Byblos and Ugarit, cosmopolitan ports, sheltered prosperous industries; in their markets Egyptian officials made contact with merchants from Babylon and Assur, with sailors from Crete, with Mycenean traders established along the coasts, Mitannian horse-dealers—a motley strident population coming to barter and bargain over their wares. In this polyglot environment, where Akkadian, Egyptian, Hurrian, and Sumerian were spoken, Aegean and Mittannian art products were as much appreciated as those brought from Egypt; local art and literature could hold their own against the best foreign examples.

If Egypt had been sole arbiter between all these more or less rival cities, she could have dominated the area as completely as she did her Nubian possessions. But she shared this zone of influence with others. She seems never to have come into conflict with

Babylonia; but at the time of their penetration into Asia the Pharaohs came up against a powerful rival, the Mitannians, who were to play a leading part until the fourteenth century B.C., when they were finally overthrown by a new opponent, the Hittites.

The Mitannians were one of the branches of the Indo-European migrations that spread into western Asia from the third millennium. The territory where they settled down lay in Upper Mesopotamia, but they also penetrated into Upper Syria, where they installed military chiefs over the native population. When Tuthmosis I crossed the Euphrates in 1525 B.C. his surprise attack broke the King of Mitanni's army; and fifty years later his grandson, Tuthmosis III, was to look upon the stele commemorating the victory on the farther side of the ford of Carchemish, where he himself massacred the hereditary foe. Seventeen expeditions were to be needed for the final defeat of this power-ful and elusive adversary; but at the death of Tuthmosis III in 1450 Egyptian power was no longer challenged.

For political gains, which had been the original motive of the military effort of the Pharaohs, there were substituted the economic advantages of the vast empire that Egypt was able to organize as the result of the ensuing period of peace. The Pharaohs gave proof of great political wisdom in conferring on the province of Asia a status quite different from that imposed on Nubia. Instead of a colonial administration they sought to apply a system of self-government, and imposed on the defeated kings, who were maintained in their functions, the obligation of paying tribute and accepting, at least passively, the Egyptian alliance. In some cities there were set garrisons, whose safety was guaranteed by hostages chosen from among the sons of notables. The Pharaoh, a text informs us, had the sons of petty Asian kings brought up at his court; their Egyptian education turned them into reliable allies when they returned to their native lands.[3] This system made unnecessary the upkeep of an army of occupation, which would have had to extend from Gaza to the Euphrates. 'Special Envoys', however, kept watch over the vassals and immediately crushed any defections fomented by rival diplomacies.

The arsenal established by Tuthmosis III at Memphis sheltered a transport fleet which put the Pharaonic army within reach of the Palestinian cities. Egypt thus suc-ceeded in maintaining her hold on Palestine right up to the middle of the twelfth century B.C., the Asian ports serving as bridgeheads for operations in Syria.

After the completion of the Tuthmosid conquests, diplomacy supplanted war. The following rulers inaugurated a policy of alliances. Feeling more and more menaced by the pressure of the Hittites, the Mitannians were the first to make approaches to Thebes for a pact of non-aggression. The first treaty of defence against the Hittites was sealed by the project of marrying the crown prince, the future Tuthmosis IV, with the King of Mitanni's daughter. For the first time in her history Egypt was taking part in a dialogue on equal terms with someone whom she had conquered on Syrian battlefields, but whose territory she had failed to penetrate.

Mitanni constituted a powerful feudal state, about which we still know little (the exact site of its capital, Wassukkanni, is still unknown). Its civilization was complex and brilliant, adding to an original Hurrian base many elements from Aryan, Baby-lonian, and Amorite traditions. Its chiefs or *marjanni* were all of Aryan origin, bearing Aryan names and worshipping the gods of the Vedic pantheon. For more than two hundred years, until 1370 B.C., Mitanni was the chief power in western Asia, where it played a preponderant role. At the end of the fifteenth century B.C. a political upheaval put on the Mitannian throne Tushratta, whose reign coincided with that of Amenophis III.

From the time of Tuthmosis IV (1425–1408 B.C.) we find many synchronisms between the two civilizations. After a triumphant campaign in Syria, which confirmed the new ruler in the eyes of his vassals, the Pharaoh concluded a firm alliance with Mitanni, as we have seen, by marrying the daughter of King Artatama I. Was princess Mutemuia, the mother of the future Amenophis III, as was thought for a long time?[4] If the young prince's indolent nature cannot with any certainty be connected with the presence of Aryan blood in his veins, it is a fact that he did not seem to have inherited the warrior virtues of his ancestors. Tuthmosis IV died quite young (between 25 and 30 years of age), but his death did not bring about any uprisings in the empire, as generally happened at each change of reign. His son Amenophis does not appear to have ever visited his Syrian possessions, unless it were to hunt lions. We know of only one military expedition he undertook, and that was in the fifth year of his reign, in Nubia. From his twenty-fourth year he seems to have abandoned all the activities proper for a young monarch. He lost no time in assuming the role of an Oriental potentate whose existence drifted along in the enervating world of the harem. Fortunately for him, at the outset of his reign he had married a young girl who possessed all the energy of which he was devoid.

Strangely, Tiy, who became Queen of Egypt, was not of royal stock. Her father may have been of Syrian-Hurrian origin, as is suggested by his ethnic type,[5] his foreign name,[6] and his functions. Among other offices he held that of Master of the Horse (what today we would call Cavalry General), an important post which generally, at the beginning of the XVIIIth dynasty, fell into the hands of Hurrians, great experts in equine matters.[7] Perhaps Yuia was a descendant of one of the *Marjanni* brought up at the Egyptian court in the conquest period. In any event, it was from him that the last rulers of the dynasty inherited the characteristic features which differentiated them from their paternal ancestors. His wife Tuiu, on the other hand, was of the physical type normally met in the Nile Valley.[8]

Tiy's influence increased with the years. She took part in ceremonies at the king's side, and, right through the reign, we find on all monuments the united image of the royal couple. She had many children but only one son. She was the first Queen of Egypt whose name appeared in the royal titulary and in official acts, even those proclaiming the marriage of her royal spouse with foreign princesses. For after the tenth year of his reign the king contracted alliances with the daughters of his allies on the eastern marches; and it was thenceforth that he displayed the culpable indolence which he was never to throw off.

The Pharaoh could, however, surrender to an existence of pleasure without, in fact, imperilling the State. On his succession he had found Egypt in a particularly flourishing condition; she was both the richest and the most powerful country of the ancient world. Egyptian peace ruled over the whole empire. The Pharaoh's authority was recognized from Nubia to the Euphrates by millions of men of different races and tongues, and the

1 *An Asiatic battle. Detail from the state chariot of Thutmosis IV*

2  *An official with sacrificial cattle*    3  *Amenophis III enthroned*

4  *Queen Tiy*

5  *Stele of a Syrian warrior*

6 Top: *Palace of Amenophis III at Malkata*         7 Bottom: *Entrance-hall of the Temple of Amun of Amenophis III*

8  Top: *Bedchamber in the Palace of Amenophis III at Malkata*

9  Bottom: *View of the lakes at Birket Habu*

10  *Women at a banquet*

11  The following page: *Chair of the Princess Sat-Amun*

Oriental powers no longer sought to question his hegemony. From the Delta to the Cataracts, the Nile was discharging on its banks the products of the whole world, carried by the fleets of the Red Sea or the Mediterranean, or by the numerous caravans coming from the East or Africa. Phoenician or Mycenean galleys furrowed the seas, transporting Egyptian goods to every shore. Gradually the most distant peoples received an impress of the Pharaonic civilization.

For nearly twenty years (until about 1380 B.C.) a great stability ruled in the eastern scene. Four sovereigns had the right to the title of Great King: in Egypt, in Mitanni, at Babylon and among the Hittites. The courts maintained steady diplomatic connexions and exchanged ambassadors; relations were excellent between Egypt and Mitanni on the one side, and with Babylonia on the other, reflecting clearly the interplay of alliances. The exchange of presents by sovereigns gave way to sharp bargaining deals; the whole thing, in fact, was an economic transaction. Egypt exported her gold in return for Cypriot copper, Hittite silver, lapis lazuli originating from Babylonia. She held the most favoured position as the only country that possessed gold, and the Pharaoh slowly became the banker of the ancient world.

Egypt had gained the role of arbiter in this system. She owed her rank in the first place to the might of her arms. Since the victory over the Hyksos, she possessed a professional army, to which, in time of war, foreign mercenaries were added. There were two branches: infantry and chariotry.[9] In the first, alongside the professional footsoldiers, were the foreign captives: Sudanese, Syro-Palestinians, bedouin, transformed of their own accord into mercenaries. The chariotry, recruited from the royal stables, was outstandingly the noble branch. The chariots were driven by officers who had received the encyclopedic training of the royal scribes. When a young man joined the skills of the charioteer to those of the scribe the most brilliant posts were open to him: colonial administration, court service, diplomacy, even the higher clergy.

When not conducting operations in person with the aid of an army council, the king delegated his powers to a 'great general'. And so, as the Pharaohs gave up leading their armies on the fields of battle, the armies (as we shall see later) became in the hands of the generals a formidable force of political opposition.

In principle the king was absolute master of the country, but the complexity of the State system obliged him to rely on a series of officials, of whom the principals were the Vizier, the Viceroy of Nubia, and the High Priest of Amun. His personal control was strengthened by splitting up the vizier's office, one official centred on Thebes, the other on Memphis. These high functionaries, executors of the royal will, were also the 'eyes and the ears of the sovereign'. Ministers of justice, they were in charge of the whole bureaucratic State apparatus. If the responsibilities were immense, the post had its gratifications, even leading to the deification of certain viziers at the end of their lives, as, for instance, with Amenhotep, son of Hapu, both vizier and architect of Amenophis II. After his death, like his famous predecessor the sage Imhotep, he became healer and patron of a sanatorium in the temple of Deir el Bahari.[10]

Whereas the vizier and the viceroy represented the civil and military powers of the country, in and beyond its frontiers, the high priest of Amun added to his sacerdotal functions a considerable political activity. He had become one of the most powerful persons in the land, and the temple of his god at Karnak was, in fact, a State within the State. Out of gratitude to the divinity which had fostered their arms, the victorious kings had offered up a large part of the conquered territories to the god, who received the best of the booty, the captives, and the tributes. Asian towns and mining districts in Nubia were dedicated to him. In origin a mere god of Thebes, Amun had become, through the continual favour of the Pharaohs, the richest and most powerful god of Egypt. His cult, made official, relegated to the remoter parts of the provinces his more modest colleagues. God of victories, he could have become the god of the empire, once peace had been signed; but his cult was too exclusively Egyptian, too enclosed with traditions, and it could not establish itself in a lasting manner beyond the frontiers. The power of his high priest was closely linked with the question of the legitimacy of sovereigns whose divine character was granted by Amun's choice: which meant, in Moret's apt phrase, 'by his prophet'. The monarch's right was always bound up with his divine nature, transmitted by royal blood. The purity of the Sun Blood was the essential element of legitimacy. And so it was vital, not only that the crown prince should be begotten by a king but also that his mother should be a princess of the blood royal. When a king's only son had a concubine as mother it was indispensable for him to marry a royal princess in order to gain the right of mounting the throne. This question of legitimacy was to be a thorny one for most of the Pharaohs of the XVIIIth dynasty, forcing them into consanguineous marriages, which, by bringing about a progressive degeneracy, was one of the causes of the increasing weakness of the royal power.

In the absence of a strain of pure blood, legitimacy had to be assured by a carnal union between the queen and the god Amun. This theogamy removed any doubts about the king being indeed the son of Amun and the legitimate heir to the throne of Egypt. Throughout the New Empire this appeal to the direct intervention of the god was a normal privilege of the Pharaohs, and Amun's high priest was the great elector of kings, acquiring considerable influence through the interpretation of oracles.

From the beginning of Amenophis III's reign many signs marked the change which was insensibly going on in the concept of monarchy. The king was still a demi-god, the Son of the Sun, but he no longer shrank from showing the human side of his being. He did not boast solely of fabulous hunting prowess, but above all insisted on repeating the fact that he, all-powerful king, had taken a simple commoner for wife and made her Queen of Egypt. We have here a sign of the times: the transformation of the Pharaoh into a temporal sovereign. But by acting thus he, in fact, weakened his prestige and authority. Besides, Egyptian society did not possess a sharp or rigid differentiation of social classes. All Egyptians lived under the same laws and none was a slave. The only slaves were prisoners of war and some Syrian women taken as booty or sold by Asian merchants; and even these were treated as freeborn servants. The immigration, begun under Tuthmosis III, continued; and the new labour force, mainly Semitic in origin, was distributed over the whole country by the chief of the king's scribes. These foreigners were registered as taxable serfs.

While Egyptian influence spread throughout the Near East, many foreigners in turn moved into the Nile Valley, where they gained the right of settling and of carrying on trade or banking. Cretan refugees, who had saved some of their property from the catastrophe overwhelming their island, offered the Egyptians the thousand and one novelties of their manufactures. Syrian bankers opened counting-houses. Mitannian horse-breeders taught the Egyptians their lore. Though obliged to have their names entered in the registers, all these foreigners had the right to retain their nationality and hand it on to their children, even when they married Egyptian women.[11] And they were free to practise their own religions. The foreign slave was also registered, with an Egyptian name added to his native one. From an analysis of the treaties it follows that a code of international law was effectively in existence.[12]

The large states considered themselves as all on an equal footing, and drew up frontier lines which they mutually respected. Passports were required, at least for foreigners charged with a diplomatic mission. At the frontiers a service dealt with the passage of travellers; and those who could not give satisfactory explanations were at once turned back. Amenophis III organized water police in the Delta against Libyan pirates. He set up customs houses, and all merchandise, except that destined for the king, was taxed. Economic and financial relations were established between the various powers, with trade treaties, customs exemptions, and protection of nationals. The system of international law was rounded off by a genuine code of courtesy; and finally Akkadian served as a lingua franca.[13]

The extraordinary prosperity which grew up as a result of the long period of peace was not without its effects on all classes of society. A lively activity reigned in all fields. There was no unemployment. Everyone found something to set his hand to, and Nubian gold, pouring into all purses, increased purchasing power and encouraged habits of luxury. The Nile Valley was covered with sumptuous monuments. Everywhere there rose temples, palaces, elegant residences. Thebes, now the capital of an empire, was the centre to which everyone looked. The king was the first to inaugurate great works; the temple of Karnak was enlarged; to the south of the city appeared a new sanctuary for Amun, which is still today, in the beauty of its materials and the harmony of its proportions, one of the jewels of Egyptian architecture. On the left bank of the Nile was built the New Palace, with decorations carried out by Minoan painters. The walls of the royal apartment displayed animated scenes in which wild ducks were depicted in full flight and buffaloes, throwing off the dignity with which Theban artists usually endowed them, joyously sported in the papyrus thickets.[14] Farther south, far from the city's din, stood the queen's villa, a simple family dwelling, with its white walls and gardens mirrored in an immense lake that was dug out of open desert-land for her pleasure. Not far from the palace the architect Amenhotep, son of Hapu, raised the king's funerary temple, of which only the famous colossi remain to mark the spot.

The sculpture which ornamented the new buildings was of the same high quality as the architecture. The finest limestone was delicately carved, the hardest granite meticulously polished. Everywhere in the necropolis were disclosed the eternal homes of great persons, in which the decoration was of an unequalled and perfected skill. Minor arts were as refined: ebony and ivory were fashioned into elegant and comfortable furniture, gold and silver were beaten into vases with pure shapes, alabaster was hollowed till it grew transparent, subtly toned glazes covered all sorts of ceremics. Fashions, too, grew more exquisite: everywhere were fine tunics of pleated linen, sandals of gilded and glazed leather, bracelets, necklaces and rings of gold and silver set with turquoise, cornelian, and lapis lazuli, ostrich-plume fans. Men and women competed in elegance and affectation. Festivals and entertainments were held one after the other, the days passed in the delight and charm of an ideal existence. Nobody had any doubts about the perennial springs of this state of happiness and prosperity. Thebes was the Versailles of the ancient world and Amenophis III was styled by his subjects, as later Louis XIV, the Sun King.

A considerable change took place in manners. The old landed feudality had disappeared under the Hyksos rule. The first Pharaohs of the XVIIIth dynasty resumed control of all property in land. The upper sections of the new society were made up of the high administrative officials, the top-ranking army officers, and the higher clergy. Vowed to the king's service, these privileged groups were gradually changed into a court nobility. In the same way, thirty centuries later, under the Sun King Louis XIV, the nobles, having nothing to do except to look at one another and compare their ideas, their feelings, their manners, became High Society.

The old veterans of the time of Amenophis II, rough and vigorous in their ways, acquired fine manners and found pleasure in feminine company. The centre of fashionable life was obviously the court, and we cannot but regret the lack of a Theban Saint-Simon, who might have jotted down for us every evening on papyrus the doings and exploits of his contemporaries, the cabals, intrigues, and endless small bits of gossip, no doubt, but also the pageantry of great ceremonies, the splendour and glitter of the palaces and temples, the charm of daily life, and now and then the clear-cut caustic portrait of some important character or the grace emanating from some beautiful woman . . .

While Egyptian society thus opened to foreign influences, among the queen's circle a group of persons were responding to new ideas on a loftier level. Let us attempt to describe briefly a few of these figures whose personalities still set us many unanswered questions.

There was Yuiu, whose daughter, barely nubile, had become not only the young Pharaoh's wife but also queen of Egypt. He must certainly have occupied a post of the highest rank at court ever since the reign of Tuthmosis IV. The finely made furniture, the beautifully inlaid coffers and the ceremonial chariot covered with gilt leather, which have been found in the tomb of Tiy's parents, were personal gifts from the Pharaoh to his parents-in-law, as the inscriptions inform us.[15] We may believe that Yuiu was an influential counsellor of the young couple during the first years of their reign. In his youth he had been Chancellor of the North, residing then at Heliopolis. Onen, one of his sons, held important religious posts; Chief Seer of Re's temple at Heliopolis, Sem priest at Hermonthis, he had become second prophet of Amun at Thebes.[16] This conjunction of titles give us some idea of the considerable role that he must have been able to play at court in counterbalancing the influence of the Theban high clergy. We can easily imagine that the first prophet of Amun could not have looked favourably on a subaltern, brother-in-law to the king, whose Heliopolitan title was on a level with his own.

But the real *Deus ex machina* of the future revolution, in our opinion, was Ay, at whose personality and activity we guess throughout the following reigns without being able to define them with any precision. Was he also, as has been suggested, a son of Yuiy?[17] This attractive hypothesis, which throws light on many obstinately obscure problems, can perhaps be supported, as we shall later see, by some comparisons of an aesthetic nature. It is of extreme importance when we recall that Ay lived on through four reigns. When he succeeded Tutankhamen and in his turn mounted the throne of the Pharaohs, he had been not only one of the promoters but also one of the witnesses, and the liquidator, of the Amarna drama.

If in his youth Yuiu was the king's vizier at Heliopolis, Amenhotep, son of Hapu, as we saw earlier with regard to Thebes, was at the same time Amenophis III's vizier and architect. We know the name of one of Amenhotep's successors, who was an active adherent of the new ideas. He was called Ramose; and for us he is particularly known through his tomb cut in the Theban hill of Sheik-abd-el-Qurnah. The delicacy and beauty of the reliefs, the pathetic funeral scene painted on one of the vestibule walls, sets it among the finest of this epoch. It is also one of the most typical; on its walls emerges for the first time the artistic revolution which we are to study. But the tomb was never finished or used as a burial-place. Did Ramose fall into disgrace? After the fourth year of Amenophis IV's reign we lose trace of him, and during the Amunian reaction at the close of the dynasty his tomb was partially plundered.[18]

After this rapid sketch of the main personages who gravitated round the throne and formed 'the queen's clan', we must turn to examine the changes that came about in the sphere of ideas and lay at the root of the religious reform of the future Amenophis IV.

In interpreting the legendary data and the countless religious texts of ancient Egypt, historians have too often presented an 'objective' history of the religion according to the ways of thought inherited from the nineteenth century. The distinction which modern thinkers have sought to make between religious and social facts did not exist in ancient times, above all in Egypt. No hard and fast division separated the State from religion, civil administration and priesthood, secular art from religious art, dogma from science. 'Religious feeling was at the base of all institutions, of art, of literature, of science; it inspired thought and animated reasoning.'[19]

The Greeks considered the Egyptians the most pious of men, though they did not therefore feel debarred from mockery of the bizarre deities they worshipped. By creating abstract notions, they took the step of providing rational explanations for myths, and could no longer understand that for the inhabitants of the Nile Valley the act of consciousness always occurred *within* the myth. Like so-called primitive peoples, archaic societies did not think separately of individual and community, community and nature, but saw them in a system of interdependent cosmic forces. Every natural phenomenon was always thought of in terms of human experience, and that experience was understood as a function of the whole cosmos. As a result, every deep-going crisis, which broke down the habitual patterns of existence, raised afresh the whole question of the reality of the world and also of man's presence in it. For the archaic world it was religious experience that had created the universe: every religion, even the most elementary is an ontology: it reveals the *being* of sacred things and divine images'.[20]

The Egyptians had then from an early stage set up a correspondence between earth-life and sunlife; and later they blended myths of solar origin with others developed from agriculture. The consequence was—if not the astrobiology which long dominated Asia and the East Mediterranean—at least certain bio-astral ideas, which originated from a particular way of representing the world.[21] The Egyptians elaborated not only a mythology, but also a cosmogony, indeed a sacred history. They certainly had their own ideas on the nature of divinity, though they left us no dogmatic treatise with a definition of it.

To understand the essence of Egyptian religion, we must bear in mind that it was founded not simply on belief but also on cult-ritual, and, by the nature of its historical development, on local cult-rituals.[22] Above all it consisted of the worship of the gods who were the legitimate owners of the soil of Egypt. Therein lay its principle and its unity. The cult, a State institution and also a public service, was given its life by the king, pontiff by right, who guaranteed it throughout the land by providing temples for all the legitimate gods of the different regions. The diversity of regions stood in the way of a dogmatic unification which would have debased the status of local gods proclaimed supreme in their own domains from time immemorial. Even when the monarchs favoured a particular cult, as happened with the Vth dynasty, which exalted the solar god of Heliopolis, they always left theology in the hands of the local clergy. Despite the abundance of religious formulas spread out on the monuments and brought together in the Pyramid Texts and the Books of the Dead, these latter were never sacred books in which the faith was codified. In an exactly opposite way to that of religious thought today, Egyptian dogma took the form of a private interpretation, varying with place, group, and even individual. Worked out by the local clergy, a doctrine was propagated according to the importance of the temple and then influenced the doctrines of more obscure sanctuaries. The doctrine, in short, was only the collective opinion of a god's priests, and it came up against other opinions of equal validity. Contradictory dogmas found place in the same religion, ranging from the subtlest of theological speculations to the grossest of fetichisms.

Ever since the Old Kingdom, the theologians had attempted to co-ordinate the multiple data into a single system which explained the creation of the world and set out the deities in an hierarchical series. Two main syntheses, however, came to the top: that of the solar cult of Rē at Heliopolis and that of Osiris with his agrarian cult. Fortified by royal favour under the Vth dynasty, Heliopolitan theology became so deeply imbedded in the religious thought of Egypt that the majority of local gods could only hold their own by being assimilated to Rē. The solar god emerged easily as the superior god because the sun was the most luminous of the heavenly bodies. And so, as Rē was the supreme god from the days of the Old Kingdom, Amun had to be assimilated to him if he in his turn was going to become the sovereign deity. The fusion was to appear as an accomplished fact in the Ptolemaic period when all the various gods became manifestations of 'He whose name is hidden'. That god was always the god of the solar theology with whom Osiris himself had ended by merging when he became his manifestation in the Otherworld.

This sort of syncretism, often contradictory, seems to have been almost the only form of real progress made in religious thought in the whole course of Egyptian history. Ancient beliefs and the formulas which expressed them showed at all times a jealous tenacity. It followed that the emerging antagonism between the upholders of tradition and the cosmopolitan court circle was not only social and political in character but was above all religious.

The changes in the State which had been going on during the last two centuries were, however, to have a profound repercussion on Egyptian thinking and to bring about, despite everything, an evolution in traditional conceptions. The presence of large numbers of foreigners had multiplied mixed marriages, and the native Egyptian race has lost its original purity. The royal family itself had contracted foreign alliances. With these diverse races it was henceforth necessary to develop a much more universal religion than that of Amun, whose cult was too nationalist to suit the distant provinces of the empire. An ancient local god, he had been joined with Rē in order to become a national god at the time when the Theban princes assumed power in the Middle Kingdom. The successive conquests of the Pharaohs of the XVIIIth dynasty had prodigiously enriched him. We have already stressed the ever-increasing ascendancy of the clergy over the monarchy. But under Tuthmosis IV a reaction again occurred, with a return of special devotion to venerable Rē-Harakhte, the god of Heliopolis. This was the moment when an Asian influence began to penetrate the Nile Valley and the need for a more tolerant religion was already felt. The trend developed under Amenophis III; but it had nothing exclusive about it, and it threatened neither the other cults nor the primacy of Amun.

Solar cults also existed in the civilizations of western Asia and the sun was there the principal god of ruling families. Its cult offered the very character of universality which that of Amun lacked. The transition from a city god to a moral god, the sole god of the universe, had been effected at Babylon in the reign of Hammurabi (about 1730 B.C.), when the local god Marduk became, by means of the concept of solar divinity, the sovereign and beneficent power—at a time when the lunar calendar gave way to a solar one.[23] In Egypt, the Sun was designated by a name which, without itself being new, was to take on a singularly dramatic importance: Aten of the Day—that is, the disk in its visible form, fostering everything that lives on the earth. Moret has pointed out that the name literally recalled that of Adonai, 'the Lord' of the Syrian cities, the Adonis of Byblos.[24] Under the simple and expressive disk form, the Sun was venerated by all, by the African tribes of Nubia as well as by the Asian mountaineers, by the peasants of the great river-valleys of Mesopotamia as well as by the merchants of the maritime cities of Phoenicia.

The creation of a vast empire was thus for Egypt the starting-point of new wealth and knowledge. The Pharaohs' policy and their desire for expansion had encouraged innumerable relationships with the Asian lands, and these ever-closer contacts had incalculable repercussions in all spheres. Firstly the army, thanks to the chariotry, was reorganized and became the favourite career for youth, to whom it offered a new ideal. The younger generations, often the product of marriages with foreigners, were brought up in a life of luxury which the frugal Egypt of earlier times had never known. Not only residences, clothes, ornaments, but also art, literature, even religious ideas, were transformed by the impact of other cultures. For the first time perhaps we recognize what seems to be a constant factor in history: the influence of a conquered country on the conqueror.

The isolation brought about by the long years of foreign occupation was now a thing of the past. The horizon was marvellously widened. The Egyptian vision suddenly reached out to meet other humanities, other sensibilities; we are present at the awakening of a new consciousness in the face of a world coloured by all the mysteries and all the magic of the Orient. Egypt indeed had penetrated into Asia; but Asia in turn impregnated the Nile Valley, and this conjuncture was to leave so deep a mark on the Pharaonic civilization that the latter was never again to achieve the pure serenity and the spirit of moderation of its first days. On the dazzling threshold of unknown lands, from this time onwards Egypt had come up against disquietude.

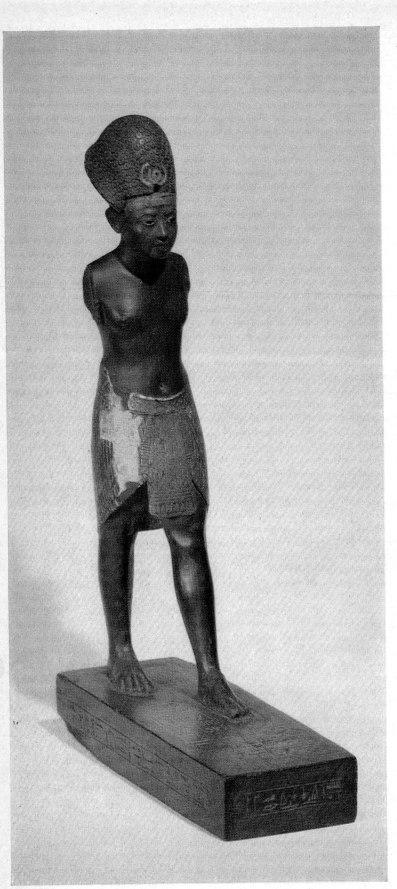

I Overleaf: *Amenophis III—a youthful portrait*
III Right: *Head of Queen Tiy*

II *Statuette of Amenophis III*

*IV Stele of Amenophis III and Queen Tiy*

## 2. WHO WAS AMENOPHIS IV?

From her marriage with the King of Egypt, Tiy had many daughters but only one son, it seems, who was born rather late in life to the royal couple, probably after the twelfth year of their reign.[1]

At the time when this long-awaited heir was born, Amenophis III was scarcely 25 years old, but had already turned away from any kind of active life. As a young man he had loved the chase and had boasted of his hunting exploits in the Delta marshes. At 18 he had taken part in a punitive expedition into Nubia.[2] But, contrary to the practice of his ancestors, he had never shown himself to his Asian vassals at the head of an army. The tenth year of his reign, when he married, at the age of 23, the Mitannian princess Gilukhepa, who arrived in Egypt escorted by '317 ladies of the harem', marked a turning-point in his existence.[3] The descendant of vigorous warrior Pharaohs changed into an Oriental potentate, a sensual playboy, whose only aim was to while away the hours softly among his concubines.

The letters which passed between the Pharaoh and his Asian allies reveal his growing appetite for beautiful Oriental girls.[4] In exchange for them he sent the gold that the others kept on avidly soliciting, the gold which they needed to finish off their palaces. Sometimes a note of sharpness intruded. When the Pharaoh demanded a second (and younger) Babylonian princess, King Kadashman-Enil I retorted, 'You desire my daughter in marriage, although no one has ever seen my sister, whom my father gave you as wife, and it is not known if she is dead or still living.' Amenophis, indignantly wrote back that the Babylonian messengers were fools and that if Kadashman-Enil had sent an important dignitary instead of common donkey-drivers, the man would have been capable of making a truthful report and of returning with a message from the princess. For, 'if your sister were dead, who would want to hide the fact'? The King of Babylon complained in turn that his envoy had been detained in Egypt and that Amenophis III's gifts were of inferior quality. 'As for the young girl, my own daughter, she has grown up and is ripe for marriage. Have her sent for.' Finally, when the Pharaoh refused to dispatch him an Egyptian princess, Kadashman-Enil replied that any woman at all, provided she was beautiful, would serve; for 'who will dare to assert that she is not a king's daughter'?

The letters of King Tushratta of Mitanni reveal even more thoroughly the psychology of these various personages. Behind the exaggerations and metaphors we sense more affectionate and direct ties, which, moreover, go back to the previous generation. Tushratta never forgot to underline the fact that Amenophis III was more amiable than his parents. He expressed sincere regret when he learned of his friend's death. He wrote to the young Pharoah Amenophis IV, 'When my brother Nimmuria died, they proclaimed it . . . he was gone . . . and as for me, I wept . . . In the middle of the night I rose up; on that day I found no pleasure in food or drink, and I was afflicted . . . If only I were dead . . . and if my brother whom I loved and who loved me were still alive, so that we might still love one another, love in our hearts . . .'

Unlike his ancestors, Amenophis III was short, about five feet tall.[5] He had the face of his father, Tuthmosis IV, long and narrow, with pointed chin; but his indolent way of life soon gave him a flabby look. His portraits as a young man show him with rounded cheeks, sensuous mouth, and almond-shaped eyes under heavy lids. A little ebony statue in the Brooklyn Museum depicts him at a later age, with his torso already thickened. In the last years of his life the sagging line of his figure was usually draped in a pleated tunic, which gave him the appearance of a fat elderly lady. Before the age of 50 he was completely bald, almost toothless, and suffering cruelly from dental abcesses. Prematurely worn out by his excesses, he died at 51, after reigning thirty-eight years. His deathmask has fixed the dolorous expression and the mouth twisted by the sufferings of his last hours.[6]

Smaller than her husband, swarthy, Queen Tiy was far from beautiful, with her rather monkeyish face, pouting lips, and broad flat nose; yet her rare portraits are marked by a pensive and concentrated expression. We feel in her a strong and even fascinating personality, with her heavy glance gleaming from under lowered lids.[7]

The only son of this energetic and intelligent mother and a profligate pompous father, the young prince was delicate in appearance. He was very ugly. His sickly effeminate body was topped by a big head with protruding ears; his face was emaciated, with hanging jaw and long nose. But his large dark eyes, deep set, must have shone with intelligence and ardour.

The birth of an heir to the throne was certainly greeted with general rejoicings; the succession was at last assured and the queen's power was further strengthened. She and her family were able to gather round the future Pharaoh and incline him towards the ideas which they themselves cherished. We can easily imagine the influence to which this ardent being was submitted by his contacts with a refined cosmopolitan culture. Young Amenophis must have quivered with enthusiasm when he understood that he could carry on the work of his predecessors, but on a spiritual plane: to the new empire created by his ancestors he would give a universal religion.

Aten does not seem to have existed as a deity before the middle of the XVIIIth dynasty. Till then he was only the seat of divinity and of the solar god himself. From the time of Tuthmosis IV the actual deification of Aten began, together with the idea of offering him for the worship of foreigners.[8] Long before the Amarna schism, Aten had a sanctuary at Thebes, between the temples of Karnak and Luxor; and under Amenophis III an official could combine the role of Amun's priest with that of steward of

Aten's Temple.[9] All the evidence goes to show that the new god coexisted in perfect harmony with the god of Thebes. His name appeared in all the domains; a company of the royal guard was named after him; the golden barge in which the king and queen floated on the recently dug lake on the left bank was called *Splendour of Aten*.[10] A final daughter, born late in the life of the royal couple, was named Bakitaten, Aten's Slave. After the birth of this girl, Tiy's age took away all further hope of children. The legitimate succession was thus at the mercy of an attack of illness or an accident befalling young Amenophis. Only the princesses could still transmit the purity of solar blood to the dynasty. No doubt here lay the motive pushing the queen, in her fear of seeing the throne without an heir, to allow one of her own daughters, Satamun, to marry the old king.[11] This incestuous union, which we find deeply shocking, settled for the Egyptians the knotty question of the royal succession. Though we lack any definite proof, it is not impossible that Satamun became the mother of the young Smenkhkere who was in turn to become son-in-law and heir to his half-brother.[12]

The marriage was scarcely consummated when the old king insisted once more that Tushratta should give him his daughter. He sent an envoy with the following letter: 'Give me your daughter for wife, so that she may be mistress of Egypt. Mane has seen her and he praises her highly.' Tushratta in his astuteness knew how to drag things out. 'This year I will give my brother his wife . . . In six months I'll send her and when my brother sets eyes in her he will be delighted . . .' In the next letter he repeated: 'To my brother whom I love I shall give my daughter for wife. May (the deities) Shamash and Ishtar however go before her . . .'

At this period the power of Mitanni still extended over Nineveh, where the sungod Shamash and the goddess Ishtar (the planet Venus) were invoked in important events. Ishtar's statue had travelled to Egypt in Tuthmosis IV's reign and once again she had to return in order to heal the king. Those events took place in the thirty-fifth or thirty-sixth year of the king's reign: which suggests that at this time the king was already very ill.

Tushratta looked round for further loopholes to delay his daughter's departure. Now he wrote in Mitannian and discussed the dowry and the trousseau. He compared them with the dowries of Gilikhepa and Mutemwia; he complained at not having received the gold statues promised by Amenophis III. Prudently he decided to hold back part of the dowry. Negotiations dragged on and meanwhile Amenophis III died.

The princess, however, seems to have arrived before his death, though we do not know if he had time to marry her. In a letter to Amenophis IV, Tushratta wrote of the joy of Nimmuria (Amenophis III), his father, at the sight of Tadukhepa and all the gifts he made her so that she might lay them at the feet of the Mitannian ambassador. Then in a letter addressed this time to Tiy we learn that she has become the wife of Amenophis IV. Who knows whether the crafty Tushratta with his continual procrastination had not been hoping for this very outcome? In the same letter he recalled the queen-mother's words to his ambassador Gillia, advising the King of Mitanni to be circumspect with the new sovereign and not let himself be imposed on. Tushratta once more asked for gold statues and complained that Amenophis IV had sent him wooden statues covered with gold, 'although in the land of your son gold is as common as dust'.

Why did Tiy fail to hand this complaint on to her son, since she alone was in a position to do so?

Did Tadukhepa, the princess from afar, become Queen Nefertiti? Doubts have still recently been expressed by many Egyptologists, who wish to see in the young queen either Amenophis IV's half-sister or Ay's daughter, though they bring forward no convincing evidence. For our part, we hold that there are sufficient clues to let us maintain that she and Tadukhepa were indeed one and the same person.

First, there is the name Nefertiti, so expressive and poetic, which means 'the beautiful one who came'. Then there is the fact that Tushratta never mentions any other queen than Tiy: which would have been a remarkable breach of etiquette on the part of a relative who was kept regularly acquainted with the sayings and doings of the Egyptian court by his ambassador, and who never forgot to refer to the queen-mother, then to Tadukhepa, 'my daughter, your wife, your other wives . . .' He sent identical presents to the two ladies: which again would be a lapse in decorum if there were some other queen and Tadukhepa were merely a plain 'lady of the harem'. Finally, and above all, there is the strange cylindrical head-dress which Nefertiti, *alone* among rulers of Egypt, is shown wearing and which is similar to the tiaras of Asian goddesses. There is further the ethnic type of the queen, which we shall consider later and which is very different from the Egyptian type.[13]

If the goddess came to Egypt in Amenophis III's thirty-fifth or thirty-sixth regnal year, we may assume that Tadukhepa came at the moment when the Third Jubilee was being celebrated together with the enthronement of the co-regent. The details of her arrival are not known to us, but we cannot resist the impulse to conjure them up.

Let us evoke first the heart-rending farewells of the young girl as she left her family and homeland for reasons of State. The princely caravan, escorted by the Egyptian ambassador Mane, crossed the mountains of Lebanon and after long stages reached the Mediterranean coast. Then came the arrival at Biblos in all its variegated splendour, where Egyptian vessels awaited in the port, ready to take aboard the princess and her suite, the countless coffers packed with jewels, the silver plate and the many presents from the king, her father. Then the fleet's departure, the coast fading away from the tear-misted eyes of the young girls; the passage over the Great Green, alarming for these mountaineers, used as they are to the goat-tracks and torrents of their native land. And then, one fine morning, the arrival at a sandy featureless beach, followed by the slow river voyage upstream into an African landscape, grandiose and monotonous, which did not bear the least resemblance to the scenery of Upper Mesopotamia. The ambassador Mane was at the princess's side explaining the curious conical monuments silhouetted against the setting sun, the tombs of the ancient rulers of Egypt. Maybe they touched port before the white walls of Memphis and paid a visit to the strange funereal domain of King Zoser and the Temple of the venerable god Ptah.

When the princely flotilla passed by the people ran to the banks with loud cries of welcome; the flocks raised up their heads from where they drank the Nile, and shrank in fear. On the deck, in the shade of the great white sails swollen out by the north wind, time drifted by in the contemplation of the palm trees and the fields of green wheat stretching on either side, between the bare mountains transformed by the nacreous magic of dawn and dusk. Every evening the boats cast anchor among reeds and payprus where a whole world of winged creatures rustled and twittered, while a kingfisher went by in a flash of blue. When the moon was full the boats could travel by night; with the winds stilled, only the murmur of water rippling on the oars broke the silence under the stars. At last, one night a distant clamour sounded from the horizon, where lights were shimmering. There lay Thebes, the greatest city of the world, preparing to receive the travellers. Soon, in the flare of torches, the ship came to a stop, the moorings were fixed, and the gangways fastened to the bank. Clothed in her most gorgeous robes, wearing the cylindrical tiara of Oriental goddesses and queens, her breasts and arms adorned with sparkling jewels, young Tadukhepa went with beating heart to meet her destiny.

Let us imagine what followed. Having heard reports of the beauty of the young Mitannian, the co-regent was anxious to go in person and receive the new-comer: a simple gesture of courtesy towards the daughter of an ally (not a vassal), but also an impulse of understandable curiosity. Before this legendary princess, whose beauty was so different from the Egyptian ideal, the young prince could not fail to be fascinated. Instead of the heavy wig worn by Theban women, which concealed the upper part of the body, he saw beneath the tall foreign head-dress a long graceful neck, a slender face with slightly prominent cheekbones, a sensitive mouth, a straight nose, and proud brows shadowing gazelle eyes. Amenophis had just reached his twenty-fifth year; he was about to become Pharaoh. In gaining power, he would be able to fulfil the ambitions which filled his heart. We know from his subsequent actions that he was passionate and impulsive. Overwhelmed now, he decided that this marvellous vision could not be relegated as a mere concubine to the paternal harem; she would be his; she would become his royal spouse, the Queen of Egypt. And so we find her henceforth at his side, engaged in the events which were to distinguish the new reign, one of the most dramatic in Egyptian history.

We must now deal with the still very controversial question of the new sovereign's accession to the throne. It appears that he was associated with his father before the latter's death, probably on the occasion of one of the old king's Jubilee ceremonies. These festivals, of which the first generally took place in the thirtieth year of a Pharaoh's reign, had the function of renewing his forces and enabling him to succeed himself. Amenophis III thus celebrated his *heb-sed* in his thirtieth regnal year, then in his thirty-fourth, and finally in his thirty-seventh, the year before his death, when he was already a stricken man. Most likely it was then that his son was named co-regent, his first regnal year coinciding with the thirty-seventh of his father. A weighty argument in favour of this hypothesis is furnished by the date of the letter of condolence addressed by Tushratta to the young sovereign and received immediately after the old Pharaoh's death in the Malkata Palace at Thebes. A conscientious scribe added on the tablet, in hieratic script, the date of its reception as being the second year—and not the twelfth as still too many Egyptologists insist.[14]

On the occasion of the coronation ceremonies, which took place at Karnak (the Heliopolis of the South), the new king inaugurated a temple with obelisk inside the court of Amun's sanctuary, in honour of Heliopolitan Rē. He had himself called Grand Seer of Rē-Harakhte, an unprecedented act, which seems to prove that he was relying on the clergy of Heliopolis.[15] This title at once put him in rivalry with the vizier, Ptahmose, who was also high priest of Amun.[16] Soon afterwards the young sovereign chose a successor for the viziership, Ramose, who, as we noted, was quite devoted to the new ideas.

We have already stressed that Aten had owned a temple at Karnak ever since the reign of Amenophis III and appeared to collaborate amicably with Amun. But the new deity could not tolerate for long a temple similar to those of the ancient gods. At the outset of his reign Amenophis IV sent an expedition to the quarries of Silsileh, under the command of his most outstanding courtiers, to superintend the extraction of stone for the construction of a new sanctuary.[17] This was to be called Gem-Aten, but was now to be situated outside Amun's precincts, in a quarter of the town which hence-forth was to be named 'Splendour of Aten the Great'. And soon the Pharaoh demanded that the capital itself should take the name of 'City of Aten's Splendour'.

Sanctuaries dedicated to the new divinity were also raised at Memphis and Helio-polis. Further, Amenophis had building work carried out in Nubia, at Sesebi, and at Soleb. These various decisions must have aroused the jealousy and wrath of Amun's clergy, who saw a good part of their god's prebends used up in lavish expenditure on the new-comer.

Thus, from the beginning of the new reign, discord broke out between two camps soon to be rivals. In the Pharaoh's camp a crowd of upstarts were active, while in Amun's the old landed aristocracy were banded together, descendants of those who had helped the warrior Pharaohs to establish the empire. Amenophis IV was compelled to recruit a new set of men, who lacked traditions or personal rights worth defending, and who therefore had no reason to be conservative. The army, however, seems to have rallied to the king, probably through a wish to supplant the civil administration and the higher clergy in the management of public affairs. Were not the provincial clergy, jealous of the Theban priesthood, also an element in the situation which needs to be taken into account? Had they not been pushed into the shadows by the gradual rise of Amun? The pre-eminence that Amenophis IV gave to the god of Heliopolis made his priests look with favourable eyes on the new religious movement, which after all was based on certain traditions of Rē's cult. In the preceding chapter we noted that the Helio-politan religion had never owned a popular character. Amenophis IV attempted to invest it with such a character by proposing for general worship the solar disk with rays terminating in open hands ready to distribute divine benefactions. This image, as comprehensible to an Asian as to a Nubian, was, in Breasted's phrase, not only a symbol of universalism, but a universal symbol.[18] A universal love embracing all living beings, whatever their country, was one of the striking features of Aten. Such religious cosmopolitanism could never have been conceived before the XVIIIth dynasty; it was linked with the new geographical horizon of the Egyptians and their connexions with foreign civilizations. Unlike the old religion, in which a prominent place was taken by the preoccupation with good and evil, the new religion did not seem to have any moral concern. Aten was simply the creative god, and Maat, daughter of Rē, personified at this juncture, not so much Truth and Justice, as Sincerity understood as an expression of Freedom. Amenophis III had already underlined his link with her by taking the names Neb-Maat-Rē (Lord of Truth) and Kha-em-Maat (He who appears in Truth). His son was to give her a yet more important place by making her into a real deity.

Present in all things, Aten, universal demiurge, had no need of statues to which homage must be paid. Offerings, especially of fruits and flowers, were made directly to him. His sanctuary was no longer a sombre and mysterious place; it was a court open to the sky which the god visited in person by flooding it with his rays. Both pontiff and poet, the king alone comprehended the doctrine; he it was who interpreted and transmitted it to the faithful. In this role he was helped by Queen Nefertiti, who was always represented by his side when he performed his religious functions. The Pharaoh had, however, created a special priesthood, whose high priest bore the Heliopolitan title of 'Chief of the Seers' or 'He who sees the Great One'.[19]

The new spirit did not show itself only in religious and social changes; we now see it suddenly bursting out in official art. The extraordinary colossi which adorned the court of the new temple were in total contrast with traditional canons. The idealized mannerism of the previous reign gave way to a brutal expressionism which must have shocked contemporaries. For a long time these strange statues were interpreted as an awkward trial by inexperienced artists, whereas on the contrary they reveal a consummate control of volume, a mastery of style which attains by deliberate excess a shattering greatness and profundity, and surpasses the ideal beauty of earlier times by its expressive force. Was it the new proselytism on behalf of Maat, Truth, which drove Amenophis IV, 'Living in Truth', as he was soon to be called, to have himself represented just as he really was? Still, the attitude of deliberate exaggeration went beyond simple realism in order to achieve a truly 'sublimated' expressionism in which the royal and the divine person were fused. Everywhere, on the breast, on the arms, Aten's cartouche marks the state of passionate possession which evokes prophetically the burning words of the Song of Songs: 'Set me as a seal upon thy heart, a seal upon thy arm, for love is strong as death.' From the outset this sudden new direction given to official art revealed how much the revolution was based on the king's personality. He was its inspiration; it was to flourish only because of him; and the two were to die together.

Another trend to which Aten gave a new impetus was the love of Nature always latent in the Egyptian character. The Sun was a universal god; his cult, impregnated with love of truth, found its expression above all in religious hymns and in art. The private tombs, which riddled with their cells the hills bordering the Theban plain, showed, even before Tuthmosis IV's reign, a supple style in which freedom and fresh-ness of inspiration produced works full of animation and of traits taken straight from life, in an almost impressionist manner.[20] By reason of its more direct technique, painting lent itself to these familiar accents, these spontaneous gestures. In advance of the sculptors, painters set themselves to observe nature and attempted to catch momentary attitudes. Once freed from the official academic conversations, sculptors, too, were to have little trouble in capturing a natural effect.

Under Amenophis III, however, a reversion to classicism took place. Painting and sculpture attained an unprecedented purity and delicacy. Reliefs of this period are per-haps the most perfect in Egyptian art. In Ramose's tomb, begun towards the close of the reign, the refined elegance and the melancholy grace of the representations belong to a civilization at its zenith and already verging on its inescapable decline. Seated side by side, with flowers in their hands, these men and women are the embodiment of an ideal of eternal beauty, but they seem lifeless, frozen into the exquisite perfection of the relief where we look in vain for the trace of some retouching or a clumsy chisel-mark, the defect that would infuse the work with a breath of life. Yet it is in the same tomb that once again there is strikingly found the tangible sign of a revolution in aesthetic conceptions. As we consider the two scenes of homage, we can sum up at a glance the opposed positions. On the left we see Ramose bringing a floral offering to Amenophis IV seated under a canopy beside the goddess Maat; the figures are in the traditional Theban style and spirit. On the right we see Ramose receiving golden collars from the royal hands. There is a subtle difference here which underlines the 'democratization' of relations between royalty and subject. The king, who is still called Amenophis, is now shown, not in the company of a goddess, but with Queen Nefertiti. Instead of receiving, he gives; instead of being seated in majesty under a dais, he and his wife both lean over a balcony, the open cornice of which lets through the rays of Aten. Here is the earliest example of a scene that we find repeated to the point of boredom in the hypogea of Amarna. In the group which depicts Ramose accepting the homage of courtiers and foreigners, the change is even more spectacular: the vizier has an elongated head, entirely shaven, with a lean prognatous profile that reproduces in every feature the characteristic physiognomy of the sovereign. The draughtsmanship is of a remarkable quality, neither unskilful nor caricatural; instead of imitating nature, it offers a new formal stylization, expressionist rather than naturalistic.[21]

These first examples of the new aesthetic show that the king had found in Thebes itself, not only adepts, but also artists of high quality prepared to follow his objectives and discard those that they had hitherto observed. Apparently in a few months they were able to devise a new style in complete opposition to the official academicism, as is also shown by the temple's walls covered with representations in the purest 'Amarna style'.[22] This distinctive style was to dominate Egyptian art for a quarter of a century, not only in Thebes and Amarna, but throughout the whole country, and even in Memphis, where it produced some of the most perfect works of the period.

Without being truly monotheist (as some have claimed), the Atenian religion, by force of circumstances, was to become more and more exclusive. If the king had been content, like his father before him, to claim for his favourite god a place among other divinities, his reign would have carried on with no tragic conflicts. The pragmatism of the Egyptians had made them tolerant towards the manifestations of the divine which at times were expressed by a composite god, at times were shared out among different deities. They would have found no difficulty in admitting Aten to first place as long as age-old traditions were respected. But a universal god could not accept such concessions. In his essence he prefigured the Jealous God of the Old Testament, who allowed no rival at his side. By seeking to impose such a divine absolutism in the very citadel of Amun, Amenophis was courting certain failure; for he came up against a passive resistance more difficult to crush than any armed conflict. He at last grasped this point, when, in the fourth year of his reign, he took a decision fraught with dire consequences: to found a new capital for his beloved god.

On the preceding page:
*12 Letter of Amenophis III to Milkili, King of Gezer*

*13  Amenophis III—statue without its head*

14 *Amenophis IV (Akhenaten)*
*and Nefertiti, followed by*
*Meritaten, before the altar*
*of the god Aten*

15 Left: *Upper part of a statue of Amenophis IV*
16 *Statue of Amenophis IV*
17 *Detail of plate 16*

18 The brother of Ramose and his wife

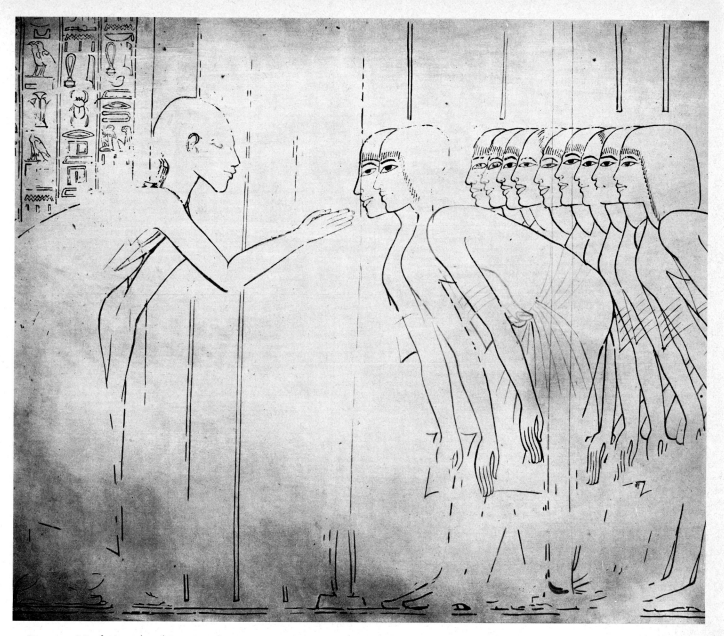

19  *Ramose receiving foreign ambassadors*

20  *Akhenaten sacrificing before the altar of the god Aten*

Half-way between Thebes and Memphis, on the right bank of the Nile, at a place called today Tell el-Amarna, there stretches a desert plain separated from the river by a narrow strip of arable land. At this point the Arabian range recedes from the Nile and forms a wide circular space about eight miles long, with extremities on the north and south marked by rocky spurs, which rise steeply over the river. Great clefts yawn in the cliffs: these are the wadis hollowed out by the force of waters rushing down from the high plateaux which are regularly deluged by heavy rainstorms. Along the wadis, since time immemorial, tracks have led to the ports of the Red Sea. The area, some eight miles long and three broad, was to be dedicated to Aten.[23]

On the western bank a large cultivated plain was also incorporated in the new domain, which had its limits defined by fourteen great stelae cut out of the rockface of the cliffs rising up at either end of the valley. The inscriptions on these stelae range from the fourth regnal year to the sixth, and announce the construction of temples, palaces, a tomb for Mnevis (the sacred bull of Heliopolis), and funerary chambers to be dug in the rocky spurs of the Arabian range. On the western bank, a little to the north, rose the realm of Thoth, god of arts and letters, 'Lord of divine Words' and Master of Magic. This was Hermopolis Magna, where, according to Heliopolitan tradition, the primordial god Atum emerged from chaos and manifested himself as Rē. Was this neighbourhood suggested by Heliopolis? There the king could find support in a clergy and population not enfeoffed to the Theban god.

Two years more were to pass before the final break. Did Queen Tiy, disquieted by the turn of events and using her ascendancy over her son, attempt to prevent the irretrievable? Or was the new capital not yet ready to receive the apostates? In spite of the *status quo*, relations between court and temple remained strained. The king made bitter complaints about the hostile attitudes of Amun's clergy: 'By the life of my father Rē, (the words) of the priests are more perverse than the things I heard in the fourth year . . . more perverse than the things that my father and grandfather ever heard.'[24] In the sixth year the king suddenly decided to change his name. Instead of Amenophis (Amun is Satisfied) he was henceforth styled Akhenaten (He who is Useful to Aten). Here was the official abjuration, which at the same time was the declaration of a political position, for a Pharaoh's name was the expression of royal policy.

This grave decision seems to have been made at the same time as the Jubilee of the god, which the king celebrated together with his own, as though to stress the way in which their destinies were henceforth linked.[25] As a rule the festival of *heb-sed* was held after thirty years of reign. Did the Pharaoh want to celebrate the thirty years of the god's existence—the period since his cult became official and the first sanctuary at Karnak was inaugurated? Perhaps there may even be something in the suggestion that the king had been born in the same year as the god.[26] What is certain is that the double *heb-sed* consecrated the close relationship between god and king, a relationship to which the latter so insistently laid claim. As in ancient times, religion and royalty were fused with one another; but now only the king knew and understood the god and represented him among men. He was the prophet, the mouthpiece of Aten. A new doctrine was unfolding, with its spiritual significance in the hymns to the god as they were written down in the Amarna tombs; we shall deal with them in the next chapter.

53

Not only the king but all the members of the royal family received new names. Henceforth Queen Nefertiti was called Nefer-Neferu-Aten (The Most Beautiful of the Beautiful is Aten). The little princesses were called Merit-Aten (Beloved of Aten), Makit-Aten (Protected by Aten), Ankh-s-n-pa-Aten (She who Lives by Aten); and the girl yet to be born was to bear the same name as her mother, though to avoid confusion she was called Little Nefer-Neferu-Aten. It is an odd fact, however, that the last two princesses, born also in Amarna, bore the name, not of Aten, but of the god Rē.

Amun's clergy had to submit, with increasing discontent, to all the innovations which definitely stripped them of their power over the throne. The king's harsh decision, dictated as it was by anger and resentment, suggests that perhaps they had made an open rebellion. Anyhow, scarcely were the Jubilee festivals silent, when repression broke out. Everywhere, by royal order, the images of the god Amun were destroyed. Hardly any monument, temple, tomb, statue, statuette, even the smallest object, escaped systematic mutilation. Even in the necropolis, on the walls of the funerary chapels, in the depths of the sepulchral vaults, everywhere the divine hieroglyphs were savagely hammered out. The zeal of the iconoclasts made them climb to the top of obelisks, to cut the shameful name out of the royal cartouches; even those of the late king were not spared. Soon the blind fanaticism attacked the names of other gods as well, and the Pharaoh was led into declaring war against 'the thousand gods of Egypt'. The persecution was, however, motivated rather by the needs of the moment than by dogmatic reasons.

Only the popular religion of Osiris was still tolerated, though his name was never mentioned. The Osirian paradise, a compensation for social inequalities, had little interest for those in the king's circle; for it was by proximity to him, and by his favours, that they were now to gain immortality.

To understand the violence of what had been done, we must keep in mind that the name had an essential value for the Egyptian. For him it was a living thing, pregnant with meaning. To efface the name of a god or a man was indeed to annihilate him.

We are told nothing of what happened to Amun's priests; but we may presume that they were pitilessly hunted down, banished, reduced to servitude. Amun's possessions returned to the royal treasury, and the subordinate staff (slaves, singers, dancers) were put on the king's household list. The god's land became once more 'Pharaoh's Fields'. So Aten's clergy were not the ones who derived a direct profit from the revolution. The king, as 'first prophet of Aten', had henceforth under his own immediate authority the administration of the god's property; the State within the State was a thing of the past.

While these dramatic events went on in Egypt, the political situation in the Near East was far from being stable. The letters found at Amarna reveal the slow disintegration of the Egyptian provinces, brought about by the culpable indifference of the Pharaohs towards Oriental matters.

We have seen that from Amenophis III's reign Egyptian power was recognized by its allies and a state of perfect balance was established between the four Great Kings who shared the hegemony. No longer needing recourse to war, Pharaonic policy held the Asian empire together by alliances. We have stressed the friendly relations between the Pharaohs and the rulers of Mitanni and Babylon. The connexions with the King of the

Hittites, no doubt because of the great distance between the two realms, had not reached the same level of cordiality; but as yet there was no hostility.

Like the Mitannians, the Hittites were a people of Indo-European origin, who appeared in the Near East early in the second millennium B.C. They had gradually extended their domination in Anatolia and made incursions into the north of Syria, seeking to gain control of the routes communicating with Assyria and Babylonia, which so far the Mitannians held. It was from about 1380 B.C., after the succession of Suppilu-liumas, that the situation began to deteriorate from the Egyptian viewpoint. The new sovereign, gaining the throne by a seizure of power, reigned for nearly forty years, and was the contemporary of Amenophis III and his successor. A remarkable and vigorous character, he had revealed in youth his military talents during the pacification of Anato-lia. On becoming king he completed the surprising expansion of his country which his predecessors had not been able to stabilize in a lasting way. He instigated various incidents that upset the political equilibrium of the Near East to his own advantage and brought about the breakdown of Egyptian domination.

Soon after his accession he undertook the conquest of the Upper Tigris and Northern Syria which the King of Mitanni had just taken over. Launching an attack in the north, he passed near to Wassukkanni, the Mitannian capital, without encountering resistance. Then, proceeding south, he occupied the valley of the Orontes as far as Qadesh, taking Qatna on the way. This military circuit brought him into the region under Egyptian influence; the moment had come when the Pharaoh should have made the necessary riposte. But Amenophis III, absorbed by his matrimonial problems, did not react; and it is from this time that we must date the slow break-up of the Egyptian empire in Asia. Suppiluliumas next attacked Mitanni, but Tushratta succeeded in repulsing him and destroying his army. We know this fact from the letter he wrote to the Pharaoh announc-ing the dispatch of a portion of the booty in return for the 'help' given to him.

After this reverse in the military sphere, the Hittite, resorting to diplomatic weapons, began interfering in the dynastic disputes of Mitanni. At the same time he fomented intrigues in Upper Syria, getting in touch with two ambitious and knavish kinglets, the chief of Qadash and Abdi-Asirta, prince of Amurru. The last-named kept up a steady correspondence with the Egyptian court, assuring the Pharaoh of his indefectible devotion.

As long as the Mitanni were powerful, they succeeded in cutting off other eastern peoples from access to the Mediterranean. But after Amenophis III's death (1370 B.C.), which preceded by several years that of Tushratta (1365 B.C.), Syria seemed unsure whether she were a dependency of Egypt or Mitanni. This vagueness of authority on both sides was what enabled Suppululiumas to gain gradually the allegiance of the vassals, though he went on writing to the Pharaoh letters intended to make him believe in his friendly feelings.

At his accession Amenophis IV had agreed to sign a treaty with the Hittite king. Relying on traditional Egyptian policy with its basis in the Mitannian alliance, which he still credited with owning a considerable importance, he bothered very little about what was happening in his faraway provinces. His main concern was his quarrel with Amun's clergy. Even the Egyptians who were informed about Asian matters did not seem to realize that the situation had radically changed.

But we must not anticipate events. Let us return to Thebes, which we left suffering from the harsh measures taken by the Pharaoh against the priesthood of Amun and the god himself.

Having finally broken with the immemorial traditions of his ancestors, Akhenaten was now forced to rally the enthusiasm of those who had sacrificed everything to follow him. He had now to excite a new devotion for the innovating ideas that he set before them. But the hate and resentment provoked by the royal decisions had poisoned the atmosphere of the Theban city to such a point that love and joy-in-life, as laid down by Aten, were blighted. Not only was it necessary to leave for this reason, but also it was becoming urgent, no doubt, to get away from the plots of opponents who, while awaiting better times, found it more prudent to go underground. Akhenaten, however, cared little for such material contingencies; he was supremely one of those visionaries:

> whose spirit from the fleshly bond is freed
> and less obsessed by all the weight of care
> is in its visions half divine indeed.[27]

Driven on by inner voices, he did not shrink from leading his people by a rash and irrevocable decision into a spiritual adventure without precedent in history.

## 3. AKHETATEN, THE HORIZON OF THE DISK

Tell el-Amarna, to use the official name, is without doubt one of the most attractive spots in Egypt. The name was given to it by the first travellers who went up the Nile early in the last century; and they gave it through an error of interpretation.[1] One of the villages of the plain had been called El-Till-Amarna by its inhabitants, after the name of their tribe, the Beni Amrân, which was of bedouin origin. Visitors thought that Till was the same thing as Tell (hillock), the name used for many ancient sites in Egypt and Asia Minor. Tell el-Amarna as a name persisted over the years and ended by including the whole district. We have, however, preferred not to use it; for it leads to confusion. The site, in fact, is devoid of the kind of hillock or Tell which has been slowly formed through the centuries by the accumulation of dead towns.

The exceptional interest of the site lies precisely in the unusual fact that there is no Tell. Here were no discoveries in depth, layer upon layer (for example, the seven Troys with their stratified levels, that Schliemann found); instead, the excavations at Amarna revealed a whole city on a single chronological level, complete with its temples, palaces, private houses, shops and gardens. Raised up, inhabited and deserted, all in the space of scarcely a quarter of a century, it had neither past nor future, like those ephemeral Gold Rush towns lost in some American Far West. Born one morning, like an ancient Brazilia, through the will of one man who compelled all the vital forces of the nation to gather there and set in motion the complicated machinery of a new capital. Its end was not due to a cataclysm of nature, as happened with Pompeii; it was brought about by an act of political and spiritual suppression, in which the agents were as ruthless in destruction as the river of lava was in overwhelming the Campanian city.

The first visitor who concerned himself with the site was an Englishman, Sir George Wilkinson, who stopped there in 1824. He explored some tombs and indentified the town as the Alabastron of the ancients. He was followed by his compatriot Hay, by the Frenchman, Nestor l'Hôte, and by the German, Lepsius, all three of whom copied some of the scenes in the tombs. In 1845 the Prussian expedition published the fine engravings of Lepsius's *Denkmaler*. Between 1883 and 1893 Maspero and other scholars had the tombs cleared of the debris that encumbered them. But it was only from 1887 onwards that the interest of scientific circles was seriously attracted, when a local woman, looking for *sebakh* (manure), uncovered the famous cuneiform tablets, which, after long hesitations, were recognized by scholars as diplomatic correspondence of the Pharaohs. The unfortunate shufflings and delays had meanwhile caused the loss and destruction of a large number of specimens.

This sensational discovery resulted in official excavations. These were started under the direction of a French mission,[2] but the first discoveries of any importance were made by Flinders Petrie from 1891 to 1892. It was rather a campaign of experimental soundings; yet, despite the chancy methods of that time, it was one of the most fruitful investigations carried out on the site. *Tell el-Amarna*, the first work published on these excavations, is still, despite its early date, impeccably exact in its general data.[3] From 1902 to 1905 N. de Garis Davies undertook the methodical copying of the scenes and inscriptions in the tombs and on boundary stelae. This huge labour, published by the Archaeological Survey,[4] is indispensable for the iconographical study of the reliefs, several of the tombs having since fallen into a state of irremediable ruin. Finally, from 1907 on, the Deutsche Orient-Gesellschaft[5] organized a systematic plan of excavations, which the First World War interrupted. German experts mapped the layout of the town and its environs, and established the co-ordinates of the maps which still remain in use. Excavations were resumed in 1921 by the Egypt Exploration Society, which yearly, until the Second World War, brought to light new materials enabling us to form a more detailed day-to-day picture of the heretical Pharaoh's capital.[6] The third and last volume *The City of Akhenaten*, ready for press on the eve of hostilities, could be published only in 1951; its author, the director of excavations, J. D. S. Pendlebury, was killed in Crete in May 1941. This publication offered the results of twenty years of teamwork by the English excavators, a labour carried out in a remarkable and comprehensive way.

During his first visit to Amarna, in the fourth year of his reign, Akhenaten had the boundary stelae carved in the surrounding cliffs to demarcate the new domain of his god. In the inscriptions of the stelae, which run from his fourth to his sixth year, he announced his intentions: '. . . I shall build Akhetaten in this place for Aten, my Father. I shall build it neither North from here, nor West, nor East. Akhetaten will spread from the South Stele to the North Stele on the Eastern Mountains, and from the Southwest Stele to the Northwest Stele on the Western Mountains . . . and the space between these Four Stelae is Akhetaten. It belongs to the Aten my Father (like) the mountains, the deserts, the fields, the isles, the upper lands and the lower lands, the water, the villages, the men, the animals, and all those things to which Aten my Father will give life eternally. I shall not neglect the oath which I have made to Aten my Father for eternity.'

The Pharaoh added: 'I shall build in this place a mansion of Aten for Aten my Father in Akhetaten. In the Isle of Aten I shall build a shadow-of-Rē (a sanctuary) of the Great Royal Wife Nefertiti for Aten my Father . . . I shall build the Palace of Pharaoh (Life, Health, Strength!). I shall build a palace for the Queen. My Tomb will be hollowed in the Eastern Mountain, my Burial will be made there in the multitude of Jubilees which Aten my Father has ordained for me, and the Burial of the Great

Royal Wife Nefertiti will take place there in the multitude of years (as well as) that of the King's Daughter Meritaten. The Tomb of Mnevis (the sacred bull of Heliopolis) will be hollowed in the Eastern Mountain. The Tombs of the Chief Seers, of the Divine Fathers of Aten and of Aten's Priests will be hollowed in the Eastern Mountain of Akhetaten so that they may be buried there.'[7]

These royal plans were at once carried out; and when, about the sixth year, the court came to settle in, the city must have been more or less habitable. It remained however a construction-area all the king's reign, as is shown by many edifices which had been hastily thrown up.[8]

The new capital stretched out, without any real order, over some six miles on the Nile's eastern bank, while the plain on the other side was reserved for farms and villages. The apparent disorder of the layout was caused by the necessity of having water close at hand, to supply the wells. Probably at this time there was no farming on the right bank, and the houses and the Great Palace were erected on the river's verge, enabling the servants to draw water directly.

Once the sites for the temples, palaces, and government buildings were chosen, persons of rank could acquire neighbouring land for the construction of their own dwellings. There was, however, no differentiation between rich and poor districts. Residences of nobles were mixed up with those of civil servants, merchants, artisans. Private houses were often spacious and surrounded by big gardens and outbuildings; but later more modest habitations and even slums were huddled between the large estates. The numerous campaigns of excavation enable us to make out three distinct agglomerations. In the middle, between the modern villages of el Till and el Hagg-Qandil, lay the administrative quarter, the first to be built. It alone presented a more or less urbanized aspect. Towards the north, separated by the bed of a large wadi which was perhaps in part canalized, there spread out the merchants' district, together with houses of those who had not managed to establish themselves in the central area. This the excavators described as the Northern Suburb. Farther still was situated the Northern Palace, a sort of pleasure pavilion of a style unique in ancient architecture. A big artificial lake took up the centre of the edifice; around it, there opened out courts in which ibex and desert antelopes were kept. In a corner was a garden surrounded by a portico and a number of rooms, which by their decorations suggest aviaries. Finally, to the east, pillared halls and vestibules led to a throne-room and possibly to the queen's apartments or the harem. 'It has every appearance', writes Pendlebury, 'of having been a kind of Zoological Gardens where the King could watch animals and birds and satisfy his love of nature.'

At the northern end of the town a double enclosing wall has been found; it opened on to a monumental gate which included a window of Appearances. A palace constructed at a later date seems to have been occupied by the queen at the close of the reign; and large dwellings and numerous warehouses support the conjecture that here lay the river-port serving the capital. A similar arrangement must have existed at the southern end of the site. Half-way between this last point and the town-centre was built Maru-Aten, a second 'royal paradise', a sort of Petit Trianon where the architecture was only an accessory to the insets of water and the gardens.

Fortifications were not considered necessary for the town, since it was bordered on the west by the river and on the east by the Arabian mountain-range which spread out in a semicircle, leaving only narrow passages between river and cliffs to the north and south of the plain. The passages were linked by a path which after the city's foundation became the main thoroughfare. By an odd survival the villagers today call it still Sikket-es-Sultan, the King's Road. Parallel to the river, it crossed the town centre under a bridge which joined the official Palace to the king's private residence. This bridge was made up of two ramps separated in the middle by a platform designed as kiosk. The latter's walls were decorated with trees and flowers, and the ceiling was supported by four small columns. Two big windows looked out, one to the north, the other to the south, and served it is thought, for the king's 'appearances', when he distributed necklaces of gold to his most deserving subjects.

Beyond the bridge, coming from the south, the royal road skirted on the left the walls of the official Palace. On the right were the King's Gardens, the temple storehouses, and finally the huge enclosure of Aten's Great Sanctuary. The last-named rose within a vast rectangle nearly half a mile long and over three hundred yards broad. It is more than probable that as a first step the king had consecrated the area itself to the god. Indeed, the remains of a small chapel of unbaked bricks, with the foundations still visible near the great entrance pylon, would seem to prove this point. The temenos and the sanctuary were constructed later, between the years six and nine, in the eastern end of the consecrated space. Then, in the ninth year, between the first pylon and the sanctuary, there was built a series of buildings, the different elements of which we have been able to reconstruct from the pictures drawn in the tombs. These structures were very unlike the usual Egyptian temples; for they were built without roofs. They were the Par-haf of House of Rejoicing, and the Gem-Aten or the Meeting with Aten,[9] a succession of courts separated by pylons and occupied by countless offering-tables. Outside, on each side of these buildings, a large number of such tables, but in brick, were doubtless kept for persons not allowed entrance into the temple itself. The sanctuary was a detached structure, without communication with the buildings just described. It stood over nine hundred feet beyond the Gem-Aten. A pylon rose in front of the first rectangular court; a second court, also with its pylon was, bisected by a tree-lined road and led on to a third pylon which gave access to the temple proper. In the depths of a court filled with small altars there rose up, before a fourth pylon, a portico with four big statues of the king. On the north he was shown with the red crown; on the south he wore the high white crown. Beyond the pylon one came into a vestibule where another entry trickily led into the final court, exactly like that of Gem-Aten for which it must have served as model. At the back of the sanctuary, but unconnected with it, there stood the great altar which Akhenaten had had raised up on his arrival and which was doubtless preserved out of a feeling of piety.

Between the sanctuary and Gem-Aten, inside the temenos, was built the slaughter-house for sacrificial animals. To east of it a stele and a colossal seated statue of the king were set up. On the same level and to the north, overlapping the wall of the temenos, was the pavilion of foreign tributes. The purpose of this small building is clarified by a representation in the tomb of Huya, Queen Tiy's chamberlain. The king and the queen

*21   Aerial view of El-Amarna*

22  *Landscape at El-Amarna*

23  Right: *Boundary stele at El-Amarna*

24  Top: *Ruins of the North Palace at El-Amarna*

25  Bottom: *The building housing the archives at El-Amarna*

26  *Aerial view of El-Amarna*

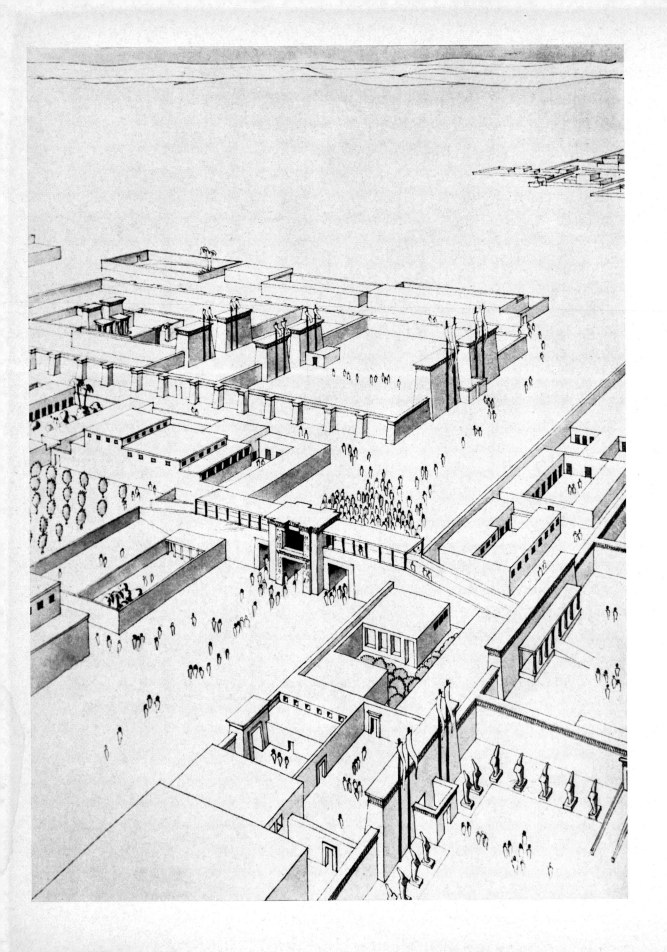

28 *Ladies of the Court in a chariot, following in the royal train*

27 Left: *Reconstruction of the living quarter of El-Amarna*
29 Below: *Reconstruction of the Great Temple of El-Amarna*

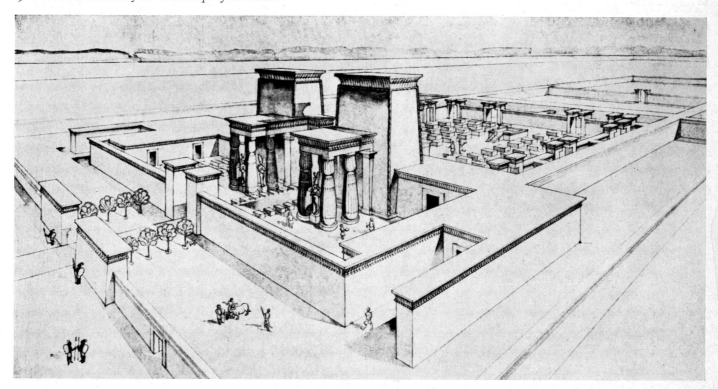

*30  Ruins of the house in which General Ramose lived*

31 *Foreign musicians with bandaged eyes*

32 *Preparing the royal barge*

33 Harnessed horses

34 *Akhenaten's daughter taking a meal. A sculptor's sketch*

36  The burial of Makitaten; mourning over the corpse

37  *Courtier before the royal pair*

38  Top: *The King bringing an offering*

39  Below: *Court ladies at an official ceremony*

40  *The hand of Akhenaten*

came here in a palanquin to 'receive the tribute of Syria and Nubia, of the west and of the east, of all the lands and the isles in the middle of the sea, sending tribute to the king seated on the GREAT THRONE OF AKHETATEN TO RECEIVE THE TRIBUTES OF EVERY COUNTRY and to give them the breath of life'.[10] This ceremony took place in the twelfth year on the occasion of a visit made by the queen-mother. The place was wonderfully suited for the assembling of large crowds on the dried-up bed of the wadi that bordered the great temple. Even the position of the temple conferred symbolic value on the ceremony; the tributes were presented to the sovereigns seated beneath the northern portico of the pavilion, which dominated the wadi. After the king had dedicated them to his god, they were deposited on the plat-forms before being carried off into the Temple storehouses.

Facing the great Temple, on the other side of the royal road, lay the official palace. Petrie was the first to dig there, and he removed the great painted pavement that is now in the Cairo Museum. The part situated in front of the Temple has been destroyed by tillage; but it probably possessed an entrance through which the royal procession passed when on its way to Per-hai. The palace was a vast complex of huge courts and of great reception-halls which scarcely left any room for private apartments. The wing that stretched eastward included the servants' quarters, the royal harem, and the Palace storehouses. Almost certainly a similar wing existed on the west, bordering the Nile, but it has completely disappeared. This part must also have had an embarkation quay, with direct access from the palaces to the royal *dahabieyh* permanently anchored there. Perhaps here, too, were the apartments of the eldest princess after her marriage with the co-regent Smenkhkere, while a coronation-hall was being built for him to the south of the Palace.[11]

Unlike his own father, whose Malkata Palace had been composed of mudbricks, Akhenaten had his official edifice constructed in carefully fitting stone-blocks and decorated it with numerous statues cut from hard stone. The luxury of the decoration was something new: even the capitals of the columns in the great reception-halls were set with gold and glazes in the cloisonné technique usually employed by jewellers. With the walls ornamented by sculptures in different-coloured stones and the painted pave-ments completing the decoration, the effect in the half light must have been stupendous. But these buildings were razed during the Amunian reaction and nothing left but debris. Only the plan, still perceptible on the ground, enables us to gather an approximate idea of the colossal proportions and the complexity of a construction made to impress the populace.

In the centre of the Palace, perpendicular to the main axis, a series of courts opened out and led towards the bridge straddling the royal road and allowing no one to pass directly from the Palace to the private residence of the king. The latter, built on a rise slightly above the neighbouring buildings, was divided into three parts: garden, house, and storehouses. Near the bridge a gradient led to a court which overlooked the garden, the house, and the stables: through here it was that carriages entered. The garden itself stretched northward to a great gateway which was reached between flowerbeds and rows of trees. On the west the vegetable gardens and the gardeners' toolsheds were tucked away on two lower-level terraces. The house itself was divided into several

sections. Near the entrance were the servants' quarters, separated from the royal apart~
ments by a group of courts and rooms, three of which seem to have been kept for the
king's bodyguard. The private apartments included a pillared vestibule, a living~room
with forty~two columns, and a private chapel. South of the chapel a large corridor
linked the living~room to a vast courtyard, and joined together the rooms of the royal
suite: a big bedroom, a boudoir, a bathroom, and a privy, the entries to which were
masked by screens of brick. The room preceding the bedroom was decorated with the
celebrated picture discovered by Petrie, a fragment of which survives in the Ashmolean
Museum; it represents the royal couple face to face, the king seated and the queen at his
feet on an embroidered cushion, with the six young princesses around them. The whole
residence was decorated with lively scenes, and the ceilings, painted in yellow, showed
ducks and other aquatic birds flying in all directions.

Separated from the main residence by a large court, there stood a pavilion which held
six small alcoved rooms: the six night~nurseries of the princesses.

We no longer are dealing with a royal palace but with a simple home, undoubtedly
rather luxurious, though domestic in its conception, as we see by the intimacy of the
apartments where the life of a closely united family was passed. The setting illustrates
the words of the royal oath, 'How happy is my heart in the queen and her children', and
the love of the ruler for his beautiful wife whom he called 'mistress of his happiness',
'lady of grace', 'beauteous of countenance'. This marital and paternal felicity did not
shrink from displaying itself, and serving as a general example. It was the image of the
new ardour that needed to extend not only to the god but to all living beings.

Close to the royal residence and immediately south, was the Hat~Aten, the Castle of
the Aten, the sanctuary normally used by the royal family. From the entry one could
already see a brick chapel flanked by rows of offering~tables. At the farther end of the
temenos the sanctuary itself was exactly like that of the great Temple; its walls were of
stone~rubble encased by two walls of cut stone. The building, like the others, was razed
to the ground, and now there remains only the line of its foundations in the original bed
of plaster, enabling us to make out the plan. South of Hat~Aten were grouped the
houses of the priests, the Temple's storehouses, and the sacred lake.

Two other roads, parallel to the royal road and joined to it by small alleys, ran
through the residential quarter. Here, south of the official district, the first houses were
built. The work was most likely carried out by contractors; for, though a few variations
appear, these houses were all constructed on the same plan. Only the proportions dif~
fered, according to whether the places were meant for large or small families.[12]

Entirely composed of mudbrick, the Amarna house was almost square, with the
exception of the porter's lodge which jutted out near the entry and was usually situated
on the northern side, preceded by a stairway or a ramp. It opened on to a first vestibule,
which led into a pillared hall where the ceiling was supported by a varying number of
wooden columns on stone bases. In luxurious houses the doors were set in stone frames
bearing the name and portrait of the owner. From the great hall one had access to the
central room, which was higher than the rooms surrounding it, so that daylight could
come in through clerestories. This was the living~room, invariably containing the
'divan' (or raised dais), sometimes a lustration slab on which stood an amphora of fresh

water, or the small family altar; sometimes also a brazier sunk in the ground. Four wooden columns were supported by stone bases high enough to form a circular bench. In the larger houses a second vestibule opened out westward for use on winter days, while the north vestibule, which never received the sun, was used in summer. Other doors opened on to stairways leading up to the roof, or on to wall-cupboards, and finally to the private apartments. The latter comprised a small living-room reserved for women (often separated from the central living-room by a mere curtain so that they might listen unseen to what was going on) and, invariably set against the southern wall, one or two alcoved bedrooms and their usual adjuncts. Private houses never had harems, and the more modest examples had only one bedroom. Children and concubines presumably lodged on the roof, where, as still today in hot countries, the greater part of family life was carried on. Sometimes, in a corner, a small loggia was built where in the cool air the long evenings were passed.

As in Oriental dwellings of our own day, there was no kitchen in the house. That was situated outside, in a big yard isolated from the noise and dust of the streets. This yard included a garden, and, apart from the kitchen, outhouses, well, grain silos, bakery, stables and cattle stalls, workshops and servants' quarters. The garden possessed a little chapel, a pleasure kiosk, and trees planted round a flower-edged pond. Extremely well planned and comfortable, these Amarna houses were perfectly adapted to the climate and harmonized with the taste for luxury, which was something new in Egypt.[13]

In a residential quarter were set the houses of the high dignitaries, the vizier Nakht, General Ramose (who does not seem to have been the Ramose we met in Thebes), the high priest Pawah, the Master of Horse Ranefer, Panehesi the Great Seer of Aten (whose official residence was situated near the Great Temple). Not far away, bordering the edges of the southern wadi, were gathered the houses and workshops of the master sculptors. In Tuthmosis's workshop many rough drafts were found, including the famous bust of Nefertiti, now in the Berlin Museum. Immediately east of the king's residence lay the Foreign Office (where was kept diplomatic correspondence), the House of Life (the University), and finally, on the desert-edge, the barracks of the army and the desert police, the Mazoi, with many stables, grain silos, and horse paddocks. From here one had a clear view over the plain where the scarcely broken surface provided an excellent space for manoeuvres and allowed rapid access to any vital point of the city or desert. Even today we can still discern the tracks which led to the mountain-top where sentinels stood on watch day and night.

Half-way between town and eastern cliff, on a stony mound, rose the village of cemetery workers. Completely walled in, it had only one exit, which was closed at nightfall. A large house near this point must have belonged to the supervisor; the workers' dwellings, all alike, formed a big square divided by five parallel streets. They were invariably made up of antechamber, bedroom, and kitchen, with a stairway leading to the roof.

Because of their funerary trade the workers employed in the necropolis were everywhere looked on suspiciously by the citizens, who saw in them only a bunch of hot-heads. Badly paid, they sometimes burst out into demands which, as was to happen at Thebes, led to social disorders. Probably those at Amarna were in as bad a way. By lodging them out of town, not far from the police barracks and near to their place of work, the authorities could more effectively obviate any chance of trouble.

Beyond the village one penetrated into the kingdom of the dead—or rather that of souls. For every true-bred Egyptian, his home for eternity had a much greater importance than that in which he spent his earthly existence. He therefore felt highly honoured when the Pharaoh, in reward for his fidelity, offered him a burial-place. At Thebes the necropolis was situated on the western bank; but at Amarna the western slopes were too far from the town and that was probably one of the reasons why the tombs were disposed in the eastern cliff. Their orientation was doubtless no longer of significance; for the Kingdom of the Dead was henceforth passed over in silence. The king referred to his tomb in the most matter-of-fact manner. He no longer spoke of 'ascending to heaven', but of 'being buried'. Inside the mountain the dead man became a 'living soul', who, in the shape of a bird could go in or out; he received his share of the Temple scraps. The royal tomb was hidden away in the depths of a wild valley that opened out on to the main wadi. The private graves were dug directly into the bottom of the cliff, to north and south of this valley, forming two distinct groups. The larger number of the tombs remained unfinished and reveal no sign of burials. Are we then to infer that in the fifteen years when the town was occupied none of the owners passed from one world to the other? That seems rather improbable. Or are we to think that when the people deserted the capital they took their dead away with them? The royal tomb, however, was put to use when Princess Makitaten, the second daughter of the rulers, died; and fragments of a sarcophagus and of ushabtiu suggest further that it was used ar the king's death.[14]

The ordinary tombs, about twenty-five in all, resemble those of the Theban necropolis in their arrangement; but even more than those of Thebes they provide us through their reliefs with the most authentic and moving image of the daily life of their town. The Judgement of Osiris is no longer represented; but we see the existence of the dead man depicted as that which a notable would have wished to live. Almost all the burials bear the name and titles of their possessors, who recount their deeds and achievements and the favours bestowed upon them. There was the high priest of Aten, Merire (no. 4); Pentu, chief court physician (no. 5): Panehesi, superintendent of the god's granaries and cattle, chancellor of North Egypt (no. 6), whose two houses have been found in the town; chamberlain Tutu, in charge of Asian affairs, who was involved in the conspiracies of the traitor Aziru; Mahu, chief of the Mazoi, whom we meet in the police quarters; Prince Nakht, chancellor and vizier, owner of one of the most beautiful mansions in the town (no. 12); another chancellor, May (no. 14), whose tomb bears witness to the disfavour into which he fell; his name was erased and his portrait plastered over. Then there was the scribe Any (no. 23), who had been steward of Amenophis II, the king's great-grandfather, and who is seen quite toothless and hoary-headed—a faithful servitor who had known four generations of kings and kept their affection, We can imagine him telling stories of his youth to the royal children. Again there was Huya (no. 1), Queen Tiy's chamberlain, who accompanied her on her visit in the twelfth year and decided to stay on with Akhenaten. And last but not least there was Ay, the 'Divine Father, fanbearer at the right side, master of horse, scribe, Sole Friend', and so on, whom we met at the beginning of this book. Close to the royal family, he played a role which grew increasingly important as time went on. He had married a lady named Ty, Queen Nefertiti's nurse, who was thereafter seen at his side.[15] There then, briefly enumerated, are some of the king's intimates, faithful partisans of the revolution. What became of them at his death? Not one of their tombs, except that of old Any, shows trace of occupation, Ay alone survived the régime and even succeeded at last in climbing the steps of the throne.

The representations in one tomb after another are often stereotyped. They differ only in details (though these are precious differences which enable us to complete the scenes), in the degree of skill, or in the general line of composition from which we may guess at the personality of the artists commissioned to work according to the owner's preferences. Even the biographies and the prayers recited by the dead man show little deviations from the set rule. Each man wanted to prove to posterity the particular regard in which the royal family held him. He showed himself in the king's presence, receiving collars of gold, attending the great religious ceremonies in the temples and, if his functions required it, participating also in the private love feasts of the palace. What is entirely new, however, is the charming familiarity with which the sculptor represented the king and his family. Many piquant details, taken straight from life, demonstrate that the artist had personally observed the various actors and the official or private ceremonies. He had had access to the palaces and temples and even the king's harems, so much so that the meticulous depiction of the buildings has been of much help to excavators when the remains on the actual site were insufficient.

The most usual scene shows the royal family in a chariot on their way to or from the Great Temple. The king holds the reins negligently and turns towards the queen as though about to kiss her, while she, clinging with both hands to the handles cut out of the vehicle's frame, lifts her face towards her spouse; in front of them mischievous little Maritaten prods the rumps of the frisky ostrich-plumed stallions with a small stick. Sometimes the three daughters, each in her own chariot, follows the parents, surrounded by guards running alongside. At the Temple they are all welcomed by the priests and a group of blind harpists; the king ascends the altar with the queen to make precious offerings to the god, while the three princesses, one behind the other, shake sistra.[16]

One of the most delightful scenes is that of the banquet given in the queen-mother's honour. The old sovereign sits on a ceremonial chair; next to her is her daughter Bakitaten, to whom she offers a dainty; facing them both are Akhenaten and Nefertiti accompanied by their two eldest girls. Before each guest is a stand laden with dishes. A number of persons are present at the feast, servants are busy with the service, and Egyptian and Asian musicians play various instruments. While Nefertiti does her best to swallow gracefully a whole chicken, the king, quite unembarrassed, gnaws away at a huge ox-bone. It is odd that a civilization so refined in many details of daily life has kept troglodytic habits in its table manners and never thought of inventing the fork. Thirty centuries and straightlaced Madame de Maintenon were needed before this implement turned up on the table of another Sun King.[17]

One of the best-preserved tombs is that of Mahu (no. 9), which is also one of the most interesting. It shows the chief of police at his duties, supervising the victualling of frontier posts or paying attention to the report of subordinates who tell him of some incursion by desert tribesmen. Mahu stands there, leaning on his staff in front of a brazier fire which a servant is blowing up; his chariot, held by a coachman, is waiting; he mounts and is driven off at the gallop, while policemen follow and run at his side. The next scene shows him bringing three handcuffed offenders before the vizier and the council of notables. They are nomads, and Mahu asks the vizier to cross-examine the suspects ('agitated by some foreign power') while the vizier expresses his admiration for the smart capture.[18]

The dialogues are often vivacious. In Ay's tomb (no. 25), the finest in the whole necropolis, the Divine Father and his wife receive golden collars from the sovereigns' own hands. This is the only instance of a women being honoured at a ceremony. We can thus get some idea of the couple's importance and their degree of intimacy with the royal family. During the ceremony, which takes place inside the palace, the sentinels and the passers-by outside have a chat on the reason for the hubbub. 'Whom is all this rejoicing about, my lad?' Reply: 'The rejoicing is for Ay the Divine Father and for Ty. They have been made people of god.' The sentinel adds sententiously, 'You'll see. They are the wonders of the age.' Another guard calls to an urchin, 'Hurry up, go and see the rejoicing. I mean see who it is and come back full speed.' The child runs off with a shout, 'I'm off, look at me.' A young man hands over a bag and a stool to a companion, asking him to keep an eye on them while he goes and finds out what is on. 'Don't be too long,' says the other, 'or I'll keep them all too well, my lad.'[19] These small familiar phrases which accompany the scenes and bring them to life makes us think of the words coming out of the mouths of characters in our comic strips.

But even more than the remarks, the attitudes are extraordinarily alive. We see the notables leaning on their long staffs with an air of importance, the gestures of the open hand punctuating conversations, the peasant woman seated on a big hamper discussing things with a young ass-driver, the coachman leant carelessly against his chariot, the dog sitting close to his master. The result is at times a caricature, but one free of malice. The acuteness of observation is not confined to Amarna times; it belongs to the very character of the people. Already in the mastabas of the Old Kingdom we can pick out many naive and good-humoured traits that are still those of the fellahin today.

But there are not only ingenuous or picturesque scenes from which death is absent. A tragic note is struck as well, and it is expressed more than once by the most human of the folk at Amarna, Akhenaten himself. After the death of his second daughter, he wanted his grief to be cut for eternity on the walls of her tomb, which has been found several miles fron the plain in the wild solitude of one of the wadis in the Arabian range. It had been dug for the royal couple at the very beginning of the town's occupation, when, a little while after the birth of their sixth and last daughter, the little Princess Makitaten died: the first could darkening the elegiac image of the Amarna paradise.[20]

The tomb, it seems, was never finished. Only a few rooms were decorated, though most of the scenes were sketched, lightly, in the damp stucco. In one of the rooms we see the usual scene of offerings: the king and queen, followed by the two princesses, are depicted in the exaggerated expressionist style typical of the first years of the reign, Even the queen has the prognathous profile that is usually given only to the king and his daughters; and exceptionally she wears the complicated crown, a most elaborate construction, which Queen Tiy wore in the official ceremonies of the previous reign. The most interesting representations occur in the small chambers consecrated to Makitaten. The scene of offerings shows the entire population and representatives of the different races of the empire, Libyans, Negroes, Asians, taking part in the act of adoration; even the desert animals turn towards the rising sun and celebrate it in their own way. Here we meet the most complete illustration of the religious hymns composed by the king to the glory of his god. Then, in the last chamber, come the funeral rites. The king and queen, followed by professional mourners of both sexes, lament before the stretched-out body of their daughter. Among the persons present we recognize an old man, perhaps Ay, and a baby held in a woman's arms, doubtless the little Nefer—Neferu-Rē. The dead girl's sisters express their grief with the same moving restraint as their parents. In contrast, the professional mourners do not fail to dramatize their sorrow in pathetic poses, which are drawn with great freedom of touch. The masterpiece, of which little remains today, must have been a life-size frieze in which the stricken group of mourners was unrolled like an immense funeral counterpoint on the walls of the chamber.

Each burial-place possessed at least one copy of the hymns composed in Aten's honour. Most copies were incomplete and often incorrect in their literary form: perhaps the work of copyists with erratic memory and faulty spelling. The best texts are those found in Ay's tomb—and this for a good reason: he was both scribe and priest, He must have thoroughly scrutinized in every detail the preparation of his tomb and the engraving of the inscriptions. Perhaps he was even the author of the poems. By his intellectual training he was perfectly capable of transcribing in a literary and permanent form the verbal effusions of his master whose 'sweet voice he heard in the sanctuary as he accomplished that which pleased his Father Aten the Living God'. Officially it was the king who elaborated and taught 'his beautiful doctrine of Life'. One of his subjects aptly said that the Pharaoh 'spends the day in instructing me, so great is my zeal in practising his doctrine'.[21] As we have already pointed out, the spiritual significance of their doctrine has been handed on to us by the hymns. We do not know if there were other prayers or magical rites in addition to the liturgy.

Not everything is new in the hymns and it is certain that the authors were in part inspired by more ancient sources.[22] What is new and remained one of the most lasting contributions of the Amarna revolution is the fact of having set out these texts in the language of everyday life instead of the literary style, peculiar to the scribes, which had become almost incomprehensible to the layman.

As in art, the solemn tone is henceforth banished from literature. One text expresses to the king the hope that he will live in Amarna 'till the swan becomes black and the river flows upstream'. The king ought to possess as many treasures as there are 'grains of sand on the shore, scales on fish, and hairs on bulls'; he ought to celebrate as many Jubilees as 'birds have feathers and trees have leaves'.[23]

Free from any esoteric allusion, the religious hymns are expressed with the same liberty of metaphor; the accent, the images, the play of fancy are those of the old popular songs inherited from far-away ages and transmitted orally by each generation, 'There is no more mythology, no more convention; nothing but the direct effusion of the soul before the beauty of the sun and of nature that draws life from it.'[24] Everyone could understand these solar *laudes* and repeat them in his turn.

We transcribe here the most complete version, discovered in Ay's tomb:[25]

'Beautiful is your rising in the horizon of heaven, living Sun, you who were first at the beginning of things. You shine in the horizon of the East, you fill every land with your beauty. You are beautiful and great and shining. You rise up high above every land. Your rays enbrace the lands to the limits of all that you have made. You are Rē, and subdue them all, you bind them all for your beloved son. You are far, but your rays are on the earth. You are on the faces of men, but your ways are not known.

'When you rest in the West under the horizon, the earth is in darkness as if it were dead. Men sleep, well covered up in their chambers, and no eye sees the other. Though all their things were taken from under their heads, they would not know it. Every lion comes forth from his lair, and every venemous creature gets ready its sting, for darkness is come. The earth is silent, for he who created it is resting in his horizon.

'At dawn you rise shining in the horizon, you shine as Aten in the sky and drive away darkness by sending forth your rays. The Two Lands (Egypt) awake in festivity, and men stand on their feet, for you have raised them up. They wash their bodies, they take their garments, and their arms are raised to praise your rising. The whole world does its work.

'The cattle are content in their pasture, the trees and plants are green, the birds fly from their nests. Their wings are raised in praise of your soul. The goets leap on their feet. All flying and fluttering things live when you shine for then, Likewise the boats race up and down the river, and every way is open, because you have appeared. The fish in the river leap before your face. Your rays go to the depths of the sea.

'You set the germ in women and make seed in men. You maintain the son in the womb of the mother and soothe him so that he does not weep, you nurse in the womb. You give the breath of life to all you have created, When the child comes forth from the womb . . . on the day of his birth, you open his mouth . . . and you supply his needs. The chick in the egg can be heard in the shell; for you give him breath inside it, so that he may live. You have given him in the egg the power to break it. He comes out of the egg to chirp as loudly as he can; and when he comes out, he walks on his feet.

'How manifold are your works. They hidden from the face of men. Only God, there is no one like you. You have fashioned the earth according to your desire, when you were alone, men, cattle, and all wild beasts, all that is on the earth and goes on its feet, all that is in the heavens and flies with its wings, the foreign lands, Syria and Nubia and the land of Egypt. You have set each man his place and you supply his needs. Each man has his provision, and his length of years. The tongues of men are diverse in speech, and diverse are their forms. Their skins are different, for you have distinguished the lands. You have made the Nile in the underworld and you make it rise at your will to cause the people of Egypt to live, for you have made them for yourself, Lord of them all, because of your solicitude(?). O Lord of every land, who shine for them, Sun of the day, great in power. All the most distant lands, you make them live, you have put a Nile in the sky so that it may pour down on them, that it may make floods on their hills like the sea, and thus may wet the fields between their villages. How excellent are your

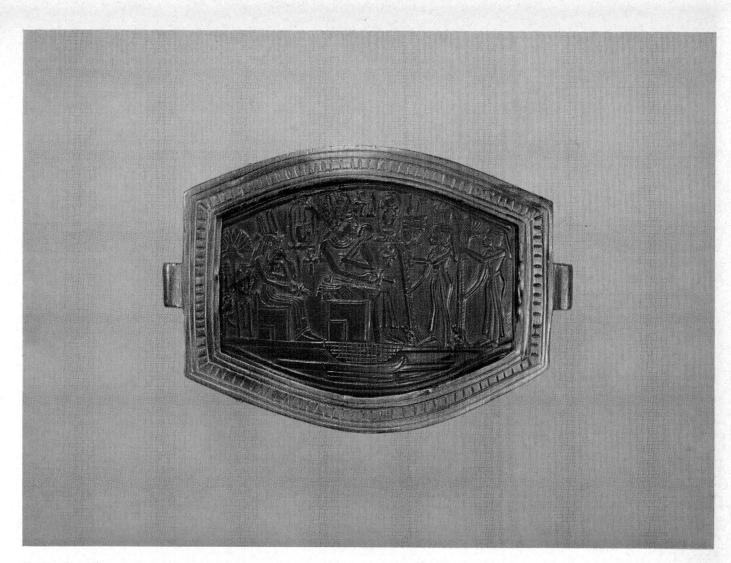

*V Carved stone from a bracelet of Amenophis III*

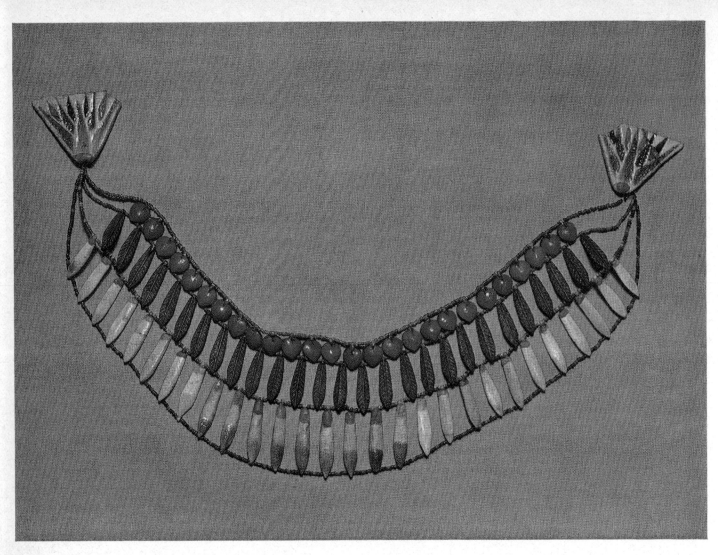

VI Neck-ornament in the form of flowers and leaves

*VII Coloured glass vase*

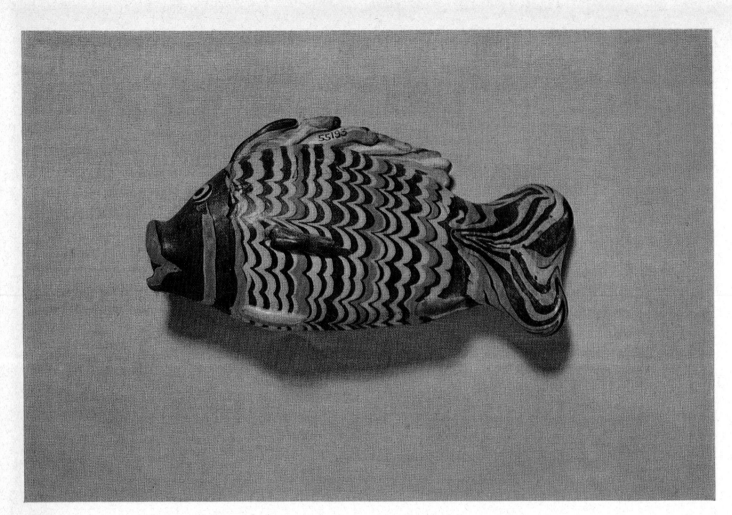

*VIII Glass flask in the form of a fish*

designs, Lord of Eternity. The Nile in the heavens is your gift to foreign peoples and to the beasts of every foreign land that walk upon their feet. And the true Nile comes forth from the underworld for Egypt.

'Your rays nourish every field. When you rise, they live and flourish for you. You have created the seasons in order to sustain all that you have made, the winter to refresh them and the heat (of summer) . . . You have made the sky afar so that you may rise there and look down on all the things you have made. You are alone, but you rise in all the aspects of the living Sun. Whether you are hardly to be seen or whether you burst out in a flood of light, whether you are distant or come closer, you have created millions of forms of yourself alone, towns and villages, fields, roads and river. All eyes contemplate you before them. When you are the Sun of day, on high . . .

'The beings of earth are formed under your hand as you have wanted then. You rise and they live. You set and they die. You are all length of life in yourself, everyone lives by you. Their eyes look at your beauty until you set and all work comes to a stop as you set in the West.

'All the beings that walk since you created the earth, you raise them all up for your son issued from your flesh, the king of the Two Egypts who lives in Truth . . . whose length of life is great, and for his great royal wife, whom he loves, the Mistress of the Two Lands, living and flourishing for ever .'

The hymn substitutes a beautiful romantic effusion for the medley of myths and legends of former times, and also for the abstractions conceived by the venerable priests of Ptah.

The ethics of the new religion still look to Maat for their basis, but the Truth now acclaimed is that of the king.

Beneath the epithets we find a summary of the whole political and religious programme of the sovereign. Instead of a purely national god he sets forth for the devotion of Egyptians a divinity who represents a force of nature, a unique god, a single all powerful creator personifying light, movement, heat, incarnating the pantheist emotion that slumbers confusedly in the heart of every human being, associating animals, plants, water and, earth with man in the adoration of this demiurge, the Providence of everything that exists on earth. We find expressed the idea of a daily creation—a new concept not to be discovered in the old descriptions of the solar demiurge.

The Sun is the primordial god of humanity. Its power, beneficial to some, terrible to others, appears nowhere so tyrannical as in Oriental countries. The radiating disk, which serves as the eloquent image of the divinity, can be understood by everyone. Further, here for the first time a king makes an open appeal to foreigners to worship a god in company with his own people. 'For the first time religion is conceived as a bond that unites men of different races, languages, colours. Akhenaten's god makes no distinction between Egyptians and Barbarians: all men are his children in equal degrees and should consider themselves as brothers.'[26]

# 4. THE REVOLUTION IN THE PLASTIC ARTS

The Return to Nature, which manifested itself in religion by the fatherly care of the god Aten for all his creatures without distinction, and in his prophet Akhenaten's desire for 'Truth', was even more definitely shown in the sphere of art. We find the first expressions of it at Thebes, in the tomb of the vizier Ramose and in the sanctuary of the new deity at Karnak. The singular nature of the royal colossi made them extreme examples in which, as much as in the religious hymns, the king's revolutionary programme was set out. He was the Son 'beloved of the God, born of his Flesh', and he was shown as such, not with deliberately idealized features as had been customary in depicting the sovereign, but as the sacred emanation of the god. To use the striking phrase of Malraux, these effigies are simultaneously 'worshippers, gods, and temples', embodying the dramatic intensity of the new spiritual ideal.[1]

On the virgin soil of Amarna this expressionist trend was let loose in the first monuments there erected: the boundary stelae, the first tomb reliefs, the reliefs and statues of the temples and palaces (of which only mutilated fragments remain), and the curious little stone shrines used for private devotions. Then, towards the middle of the reign, the exaggerations were toned down. Was this the result of a sort of aesthetic wearying in the face of the effigies that often caricature the royal couple? Or was it that several more expert sculptors were brought in, who, while carrying out the king's directives, added their technical skill and their more precise knowledge of the human body? Certainly sculpture in large part returned to the idealized naturalism of the previous reign, and the later works fit without much difficulty into the artistic evolution of the XVIIIth dynasty.

Does all this mean that the Amarna interlude was fugitive and that nothing new or lasting survived out of it? Not in the least; for without the brutal break with age-old traditions many characteristic elements would not have been able to develop and leave a mark which has its permanent effect on future generations. For example, a new conception of space showed itself in reliefs and paintings. To appreciate it, we must remember that Egyptian art, like most archaic arts, had always been based on ideas rather than sensations.[2] Essentially a traditional art, it had maintained over millenia the kinds of knowledge established at the beginning and had expressed them by means of very strict conventions from which the artists hardly ever deviated. As a result the latter had never been capable of 'seeing' outside those conventions, just as we ourselves see according to our own system of perspective, which has been taught to us in our youth. Egyptian art, purely cerebral in its outlook, represented objects as they have been registered in our memory, not as they appear to the eye.

We have already noted that under Tuthmosis IV, a certain freedom appeared in the tomb-paintings, when the artists sought to throw off the academicism of the 'books of models.' At Amarna these tendencies were no longer fortuitous, but were to be found in even the most official productions. The artists consciously struggled to express a visual perception, a direct observation of the appearances of nature, a likeness and not a symbol. The composition of the famous mural painting in the northern Palace was no longer broken up into rows or interrupted by the angles of the room. It ran continuously over the whole wall, giving a rich impression of a papyrus thicket rustling with birds. The spectator was no longer in front of the scene but was drawn right inside it.

This new *unity of composition* is again found on certain reliefs. The scene of sun-worship in the royal tomb, mentioned in the previous chapter, even shows a rough-and-ready attempt at perspective. Desert animals, beyond the temple-precincts, climb up the rocky hills, converging towards the same point on the horizon.

In the private tombs we see these obvious novelties side by side with representations in a more traditional spirit. The composition continues to unfold in different registers, but the *unity of action* is indicated by a piece of architecture or some accessory, as in stage sets. People are linked by a psychological element; and yet, though they take part in the same incident, they are individually differentiated. Not only do the artists seek to express movement, they succeed in catching the elusive moment of a gesture. Objects and beings are no longer congealed as 'things in themselves'; they have been taken from life and set down in such a spontaneous way that they have kept their power of moving us.

Again, in the treatment of the round, after the uncompromising realism at the outset, the later works reveal a balance between innovation and the latent desire for harmonious beauty.

In his quest for truth at all costs, Akhenaten had rejected that ideal. In art as in religion he imposed his ideas. He kept in touch with the work of artists and visited their studios. As the royal model was ugly, the sculptor was henceforth required to reproduce his features without manipulating them, even to the extent of stressing the ugliness by omitting nothing of his bodily deformities. Such excessive realism could not but result in the strange art of the colossi, an art charged with mysterious and primitive magic. But the Egyptians had been too long civilized to settle down to an ideal so far removed from their sensibility. Over the years the realistic and harsh aspects grew softer and in their turn begot 'Amarna' commonplaces. The artists learned how to illuminate their portraits with an intense inner life, while preserving the characteristic features; their art became simultaneously spiritual, thus attaching itself again to tradition, and naturalistic, thus profoundly differentiated from the works of earlier times.

We may wonder at the profusion of portraits of the royal family at a time when private statuary was practically non-existent. By abolishing all the divine images, the new theology showed itself too abstract for many tastes. Popular fervour had at all times been accustomed to prayers before a statue, and now showed little inclination towards worship of an immaterial god. So the people began to worship the god's representative, the king. Did the latter insist on an actual 'personality cult' from his subjects? Certainly, by assimilating himself with the divinity, the Pharaoh did end by monopolizing all worship for himself and his family. That explains the great number of representations of them, both in the round and in relief, which decorated the private altars built by each family in its garden or in a corner of the living-room.

This unusual demand for statuary, together with the new royal directives, drew the Amarna sculptors into studying their models with exceptional attention. They attempted to make portraits of them. With this end in view, they used for artistic purposes a procedure long known to embalmers—that of moulds. A large number of plaster casts have been found in Amarna, most of them coming from the same studio.

In December 1912, the Deutsch Orient-Gesellschaft discovered the house of the sculptor Tuthmosis at the corner of the south wadi and the Street of the High Priest.[3] With small differences, it had the same layout as the big mansions described in the previous chapter. Besides the main structure it had several outhouses and dwelling places, which all together made up a small but genuine estate. In the north-east of the entrance-court a more modest house stood, which, according to Professor Borchardt, was that of the figure-carver; to the south of a wide space in which was a big well, the workmen's houses were huddled close together around an irregular courtyard. This section was linked to the main estate proper only by a narrow door at the end of a passage which had its entry screened off. Here and there in the yards the diggers found debris-cluttered ditches. In one such ditch they came upon the lid of an ivory case with the simple inscription: 'Tuthmosis Chief Sculptor'. Fragments of stone and unfinished works were lying all around, so that we may assume that work was carried on in both yards, in the shelter of small walls supporting pent-roofs for protection against the sun.

The most interesting sculptures were found in two small rooms adjacent to the big hall of the main building. There, scattered over the floor in much disorder, were heads in sandstone, limestone, plaster, hands and bits of feet, and so on. Against the wall, upside down, just as it had fallen from the wooden shelf three thousand four hundred years before, miraculously intact lay the famous bust of Queen Nefertiti. When the shelf, eaten through by white ants, collapsed, the objects on it had their fall deadened by the sand which had slowly drifted into the rooms. No sound troubled the silence of the abandoned dwelling.

Clear signs enabled the diggers to recognize the uses to which the different rooms were put—to such an extent that with a little imagination we can reconstruct the crumbled walls and fallen roofs, and repeople afresh the workshops and the yards of a small busy world going about its various jobs in the warm golden light. The master, Tuthmosis, works at home in the huge hall that serves him as studio. Incompleted sculptures, fragments of stone and plaster, a drillhead as well as drills themselves, indicate clearly enough the place where he worked. As he gives his final touches to a head of the queen, his attentive pupils utter admiring exclamations: 'But she's alive!' From time to time he crosses the vestibule and goes down into a small yard where several works are in hand. An assistant is finishing off an alabaster figurine; other statuettes in alabaster and obsidian await their turn. Northwards, two sheds show reserves of plaster and stone; numerous splashes on the wall show that the moulder has worked here.

In the figure-carver's house everyone is occupied. Here it is that hard stone is preferably cut. A head of the queen in grey granite is on the way to completion, and 'to see the effect' the sculptor has already tinted the beautiful closed lips with pale rose. In the cool shade of the yard's sycamores and tamarisks, workmen hew blocks of stone or chip away with the point, under the supervision of the 'scribe of outlines' who corrects with a black or red brush-stroke the shape now taking form. In the big well with its slippery steps, an apprentice bringing water to mix plaster passes by a servant-girl coming to fill her amphora; they exchange some cheerful backchat. Everywhere resounds the rhythmic ring of mallets, punctuating the songs with which oriental workers always accompany their labours, while now and then breaks in, the harsh cry of geese that waddle about and seek for something green at the foot of the trees, or the subdued lowing of cattle that stamp in the fragrant dimness of the stables. When evening comes and the last rays of the sun gild the domes of the grain-silos that look like giant beehives, when the shadows of the buildings lengthen in the courts, the servants get busy around the ovens. One by one, the workers leave their benches and go off towards their own living-quarters, where the doors are carefully closed by the foreman till the next morning. Tuthmosis himself puts down his spatula and retires to his living-room where the ceiling is adorned with yellow, blue, and red beams. Seated on the stone dais, he chats gaily with friends and drinks wine from the decorated amphora which a servant has fetched from a small room nearby. When night has fallen, he goes to lie in the cool alcove of his room, where on the white linen-covered couch he sleeps peacefully dreaming of his next masterpiece.[4]

The discovery of a studio where the activities were abruptly interrupted by the intrusion of events from outside, is of exceptional value, not only for the study of Egyptian sculpture, but also for very history of portraiture. By finding sketches and unfinished sculptures, we can reconstruct the various stages in the sculptor's work and follow them out till completion is reached. As for the masks, are they moulds of sketches in clay, as Professor Roeder has argued?[5] Are they moulds of stone sculptures, or are they moulds taken directly from the human face? Each of these positions has had its supporters, and some Egyptologists have gone so far as to accept them all, without noticing the fundamental contradictions that set them in opposition to one another.[6] In two studies, written over twenty years ago, the author set out arguments for rejecting the hypotheses of sketches in clay or loam; and since then she has gained the conviction that most of the masks have been moulded directly from a living or dead face. They are therefore not works of art, but instruments of artwork.[7] But even if they are not true artistic creations, they are none the less precious ethnical documents. They even assume a strong emotional value when we think of the personages whom they represent: the leading actors in the Amarna adventure. Such direct witnesses from a vanished world arouse an intense curiosity, and we study them with the hope of grasping something of the souls beyond the petrified features.

It is the first time that excavations have supplied us with indubitable proof of the use made by sculptors of the technique of moulding from the life; but we have every reason to suppose that the process was not new in Egypt. Far back in the IVth dynasty it was used for the same purpose, as in all epochs where a realistic trend appears in art. Its presence *always* coincides with a spiritual or philosophic revolution, when men renew their vision of life or the universe.[8]

But contrary to what has happened in other civilizations, the use of moulding from the life does not lead in Amarna to the realistic portrait. Doubtless the sculptor opens the eyes on the plaster casts; but he goes no further; immediate reality does not interest him. He does not seek to fix the expression that he wants to render on the external anatomic structure. The hardening, the interpretation of a moment, which already the moulding drawn from nature represents, is not for him the end at which he aims; it is the point of departure towards a naturalism endowed with grace and vigour, an idealized naturalism, which will raise his art to a higher level—towards that 'second' reality called poetry. The moulding from nature becomes for the Amarna artist an instrument for prospecting adapted to the new tendencies of art.

The religious purpose of Egyptian art is doubtless one of the causes of the sculptor's indifference towards immediate reality. Perhaps, indeed, we must look even farther back if we are to understand. To the ancient Egyptians, likeness was not enough for the identification of a statue. The name inscribed on it was essential. The animist belief that the statue serves as a support for the wandering soul is common to many primitive peoples; it continued to lurk obscurely even in the depths of Greek thought.

However, in Hellenic statuary, which soon freed itself from all funerary needs, we never get a glimpse of the 'personality' behind the human representation. That was to be discovered only when, at the decline of Hellenism, a new form of human consciousness was born. The metaphysical impossibility of being concerned with personality therefore belongs not only to Egypt but to all antiquity. Though there are some Egyptian works of a great expressive force, they remain exceptional and isolated.

The possible identification of some of the moulds found in Tuthmosis' studio helps us to clarify their use. We can move from the masks, taken directly from the face, by a process of steady stylization, to the idealized portraits of the royal family. By classifying them we can reconstitute the successive stages that transform a mask moulded from nature into a study-mask and finally into a studio-model. Some examples, scarcely retouched, are simple exercises on which apprentices tried out their hand.

How has the identification of the masks been managed? Professor Schafer made some attractive attributions which we will examine in detail later on. It is here that certain elements become important; for we need to distinguish the mask moulded from a living man and the mask moulded from the dead. In some cases we know definitely that those whose portrait we think we possess were still alive at the end of the Amarna period. For instance, there was the Divine Father Ay, of whom we have frequently spoken. Professor Schäfer believed that he recognized him in a fascinatingly ugly head which suggests the mask of a Nō dancer. We are inclined to accept this attribution. On comparing its profile with that of Ay shown in his tomb, we find the same characteristic line of jaw. But we know that Ay was still alive at the time of the Theban restoration; for he succeeded Tutankhamen on the throne. The mask was then taken from a living man, as we feel when we look at it; it was retouched by the same hand as fashioned the polychrome bust of Nefertiti. The heavy eyelids with finely chiselled strokes are found only in these two works. The queen's head the right eye-socket holds a crystal eye; but here in Ay's mask the socket contains only the cement which possibly held a similar inset.

We spoke earlier of the plausible hypothesis proposed by Cyril Aldred concerning the relationship between Ay and Queen Tiy.[9] If we compare his mask with the small ebony head of the queen found in the Fayum, the resemblance of the two faces is striking: the same high cheekbones under slightly closing lids, the same strong and sulky mouth. In the queen's face, however, all these traits have been feminized and softened, while the plaster cast shows us a reality which has suffered no transposition.

Other moulds own the advantage of being able to be compared with the artworks which were in fact derived from them. One mask stands out by its slightly ironic touch of pride, though there is something tender in the irony, given away by a dimple at the corner of the mouth. The face is young, with a noble forehead above the pure arch of the brow, a firm chin, and full but finely formed lips. This rather damaged mask was exhibited in the Berlin Museum as that of an unknown man. But the features, with its sensitive charm, have nothing virile about them; the long flexible neck, a certain thinness in the contours, and, above all, the very characteristic little dimple, are all details that we find repeated on Nefertiti's official bust. The high bare forehead surprises us; for it is usually hidden under the royal head-band; but a careful comparison of the two faces seems to us conclusive. The question, however, remains: Was the mould taken from a sculpture, as was suggested in the excavation journal, or was it taken from the face?

During the winter of 1932-3 English excavators found in a studio near the Great Temple a mask that no one hesitates to identify as the queen's.[10] The sunken eye-sockets, the emaciated face, suggest that this time the mould was made after the sovereign's death. In the first mask the eye has been opened up on the closed lid; the form has thus been shortened, so that we do not find the heavy lid half-concealing the eye—a feature so noticeable in the bust. The ears are a shapeless mass (it would be impossible to mould the ear of a living person in detail without hurting it when removing the plaster); but the lobe, when we turn the mask sideways, is seen to be on the same level as the nostrils, as in real life. Small seams (of the sort left by a mould) under the nose, near the ears, and on the temples where linen has protected the hair, show us the places where the plaster has not adhered to the flesh. Slight breaks at the neck reveal the successive stages of the moulding process: the tendons are marked as in Ay's mask, in short all these details provide a proof that we have before us a work taken direct from life, though touched up by the sculptor's hand. The firm modelling of the cheeks, the flow of the forehead, betray the spatula that has smoothed out the roughnesses of the plaster. This mask, which was not intended to last, has succeeded better than the bust in becoming an image of eternity, capturing like a quivering bird the subtle and evanescent smile of her who was the royal wife Nefertiti.

One of the many effigies connected with the king is usually described as either a model or a cast from a statue's head. There are several objections to the second descrip-

41 Floor-painting: *Duck amid papyrus reeds*

42  Top: *Grapes*                                    43  Bottom: *Corn-field*

44  *Two profiles of Akhenaten—Sculptor's sketches*

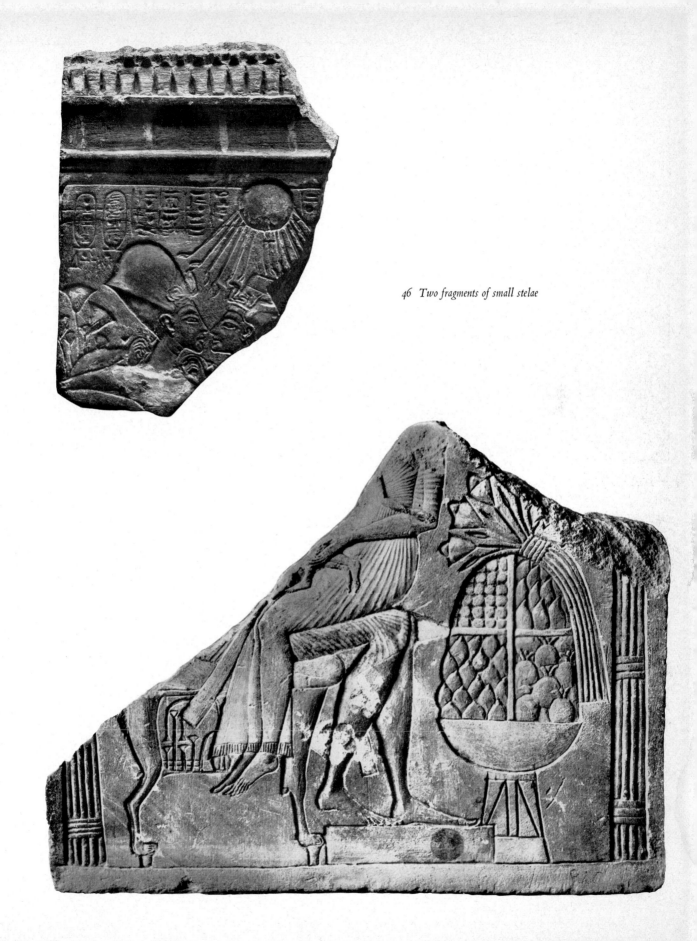

46  *Two fragments of small stelae*

47  *Mask of Ay in plaster*

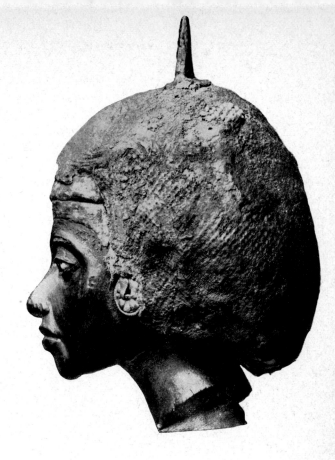

48  Profile of the mask of Ay

49  Head of Queen Tiy. Profile, see plate III

50  *Head of Queen Nefertiti (profile)*

51  *Mask in plaster of Queen Nefertiti (profile)*

52  *Mask of King Akhenaten in plaster*

53  *King Akhenaten—plaster-cast*

54 *King Akhenaten, mask in plaster*

55 *King Akhenaten—plaster-cast from a stone head*

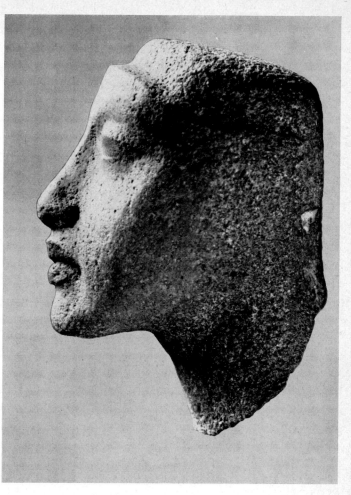

56  Death-mask of Princess Makitaten ( ? )

57  Small head of Princess Makitaten ( ? )

58 *King Amenophis III. Plaster-cast after a stone head*     59 *Death-mask of Amenophis III ( ? )*

60  King Amenophis III. Plaster-cast of a stone head (profile)

61  Death-mask of Amenophis III ( ? ) (profile)

62  *Mask of Queen Nefertiti (plaster) (?)*

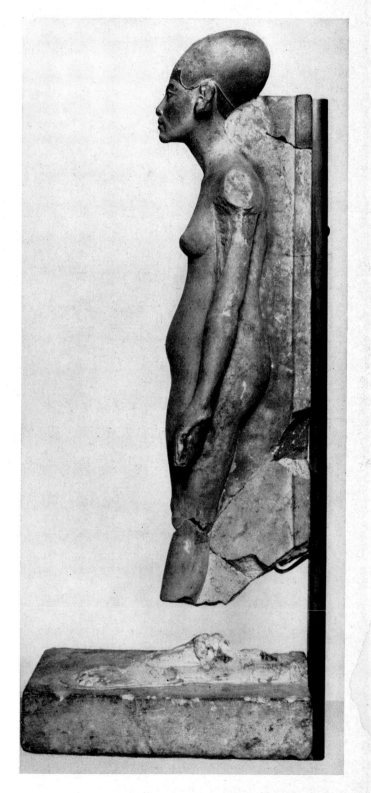

64 *Smenkhkare. Part of a relief*

65 *Unfinished head of Nefertiti*

66 *Study for a bust of Nefertiti*

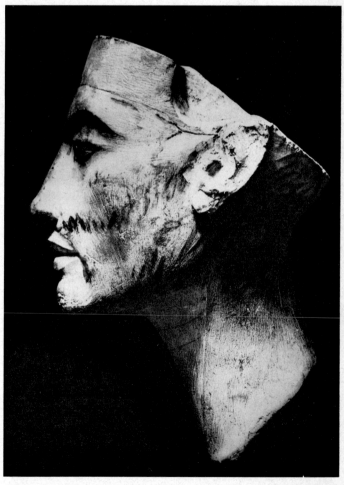

68  *Head of Princess Meritaten ( ? )*

69  *Small head of a Princess*

67  Left: *Unfinished head of Nefertiti*

70 *Death-mask of a man*

tion. The linen covering head and nape of neck, the anatomical details such as the sterno-mastoid muscle (visible when the head is thrown back), the projection of the jaw resulting from this movement, the ears set at the right height but pushed slightly down and aside: all these aspects are consistent with a cast from life—the subject being laid flat with his head resting on a linen cloth and his chin thrust upwards. In the Berlin Museum an attempt has been made to correct the movement by showing the mask leant a little forwards; but this does not affect the relation of the head to the neck. What makes it seem like a piece of sculpture is the royal headband. But if we look at the mask full-face, we note that the forehead, the headband, and the ears, have been made to stand out after the event from the general mass of linen covering them all. Besides, there has been much retouching, about the eyes, where the lids are formally stylized, and about the mouth; the skin also has been smoothed by the spatula. Are we then looking at the moulded mask of the king? Besides the anatomical details which tend to prove it, we may point to a general thinning of forms, a sort of drying-up, a premature aging, which betrays perhaps a sickly condition absent from the official portraits. The mask thus brings us the exact image of the sickening king, the image which the sculptor has embellished in those portraits. And if we have here the king's mask taken from life, it is more than probable that the Petrie mask, the one that that archaeologist found in the workshop of the royal shawabtis, may be the king's death-mask.[11]

Another mask, fairly similar to the one discussed, is also generally considered to be the moulding of a sculpture of the Pharaoh. The resemblance is strong, but the physiognomy is of a younger man. The works from Tuthmosis' studio seems all to be more or less contemporary; and it would be surprising to find among them a portrait of the king in his youth and already showing advanced stigmata of disease. But if it is not the king, would it not be one of his daughters, who alone could claim a real likeness to him? Which daughter then? The face recalls Akhenaten's features; but the softened contours of the cheeks and the roundness of the neck where no tendons show, give it a more feminine appearance, though the head is placed in the same position as in the royal mask. Would it not be Makitaten, dead before her father and buried in the paternal tomb? We possess, it seems likely, the princesss's portrait in the exquisite small sandstone head found in the same studio. Comparison of mask and head is disturbing. We see the same elongated face, the same pointed chin, but in the mask the face is emaciated, the nostrils are pinched, the features drawn by death. We feel sure that we are looking at the death-portrait of the little princess, touched up in the same way as the royal mask.

So far we have examined the masks from a double viewpoint: that of technique and of likeness. But there remains a series of isolated pieces which do not show sufficiently clear characteristics in themselves or which are not like enough to any of the portraits in Tuthmosis' studio to be identified. From a material viewpoint, nothing prevents us from considering them as masks moulded from the face. They are technically just the same as the works we have studied, and their dimensions are normal; but the work of touching-up has been carried so far that we can no longer make out those elements which a moulding taken from life should reveal. We can study them best by indirect deductions as we compare them with one another. Their main interest lies in the fact that they are transitional works which serve to illustrate the process of transforming mask into model; and so we shall call them mask-studies. A certain number of models, less than the masks, have been found on the same site. Though only a few of the masks can be identified, the models *all* depict members of the royal family and each one owns its original mask. Two models are in plaster and appear to have been moulded from works in stone. Were these unfinished heads moulded so that the studio might have in hand for use in future works the official features of various personages? The original works have disappeared, and we therefore cannot reply with any certainty. Perhaps the originals were commissions that had been delivered; and the care taken in making reproductions of them proves their importance. They were probably executed by Tuthmosis himself. Black touches on the model of Akhenaten underline the edge of the eyelids and the eye-brows; they also mark out the eyes and run from nose to mouth; a median line, still visible in the lower part of face and neck must certainly have served as a guiding line for the copyist.

The model representing Amenophis III was first compared to an unretouched death-mask by Professor Schäfer; and though there is no material proof to back up the attribution, it has been generally accepted.[12] It has even been used by some scholars as a proof of the prolonged co-regency of the two sovereigns and the presence of Ameno-phis III in Amarna. The model of Amenophis III seems in fact to have served for the numerous statues of that Pharaoh which were executed for the small sanctuary, the 'Shadow of Tiy', inaugurated in the twelfth year.[13] The model's presence in Tuth-mosis' studio allows us to conjecture that it was he who had been commissioned to make the heads.

Nefertiti's bust, by its almost perfect state of preservation and its meticulous finish, is justly one of the most celebrated works of its period. 'It is useless to describe it', wrote Professor Borchardt in his excavation notes, on the evening after its discovery; 'just look at it'.[14] Several years later, however, he was to describe it at loving length. To begin with, the work is disconcerting with its polychromy, which jars on our modern taste and seems to freeze the features by obscuring the subtlety of the modelling. But soon its charm works. In speaking of it, critics have evoked the Florentine art of the Quattro-cento; and indeed the long slender neck, the oval visage, the fine high arch of the brows, the large almond-shaped eyes, and finally the dimples at the corners of the lips, the faintly disillusioned smile, make this charming young woman into the elder sister of the melancholic and meditative nymphs of the Medici world. The sculptor has succeeded in conveying the grace of the neck bending under the weight of the tall tiara, a head-dress of which the queen seems to have been particularly fond and which sets off admir-ably the slightness of her nape and the fine curves of her face. The boldness of execution, which leaves out the tenon in the throat, has a felicitous effect; for it underlines the contrast of the heavy coiffure and the frail neck. The eyelids with a sort of hemmed edge are at full-stretch like sails, and add to the sweetness of the eye's expression. That expression is unique for another reason too; for, according to Professor Borchardt's statements, the queen's bust never owned more than one eye. The left socket was left intentionally empty—probably in order to give a lesson in technique. The portrait was not then created solely for use as a model, but was left as also a technical try-out, for the purpose of teaching an apprentice how to hollow a socket before inserting an eye of crystal and glaze.

We can see exactly how such models were used by looking at the practice pieces found near them. Among the latter there is one that looks like a preparatory stage for the bust; but on close examination we discover that this opinion is untenable. What we have is a study made *after* the queen's bust. Viewed from some distance, the proportions of the two heads seem the same; but when we come nearer, the clumsinesses of the supposed model grow apparent. The mouth is too big, the upper lip is made heavy, without any of the delicate curves perceptible in the bust. The full face is without relief. So is the profile; and we see nothing of the modelling which gives a subtle play of life to a sculptured surface. The profile, fairly well developed, has already something of finish, which reveals the link with the bust; but there is an indefinable quality which forbids us to interpret the head as a preparatory study for the exquisite masterpiece. There is nothing whatever of the lively character of a work in process of gestation. It is stiff, lifeless; and the quite superficial resemblance to the bust has been imparted before the planes of the face have been built up. This point is further confirmed by the numerous corrections painted on it by an impatient brush.

No tools were found in Tuthmosis' studio; they were probably taken away, as still useful, when the town was abandoned. But we can detect the traces they left on the unfinished works, and step by step can follow the hewing of the stone. The methods of work did not differ from those used already in the Old Kingdom. A block of stone was sawn roughly up into the required size; and the sculptor traced lines on it to indicate the general shape. Then the stone was worked with the point till the contours were entirely visible. After that the brush was again called on, to paint the details in. The chisel then took over from the point, and at each step, as the unwanted parts of the stone were removed, the paint brush again showed the course to be followed, right up to the final polishing.[15]

This rule-of-thumb technique, which was to last till the end of the Pharaonic civilization (when the Greeks introduced into Egypt their perfected apparatus), was based on age-old traditions. We can thus doubtless understand the astonishing hereditary mastery of the stone-cutters, and also their routine attitudes. Even during the Amarna interlude the sculptors never relinquished certain of their conventions such as the famous 'law of frontality' or the supports sustaining the body and the parts of a statue. At most they tried to cover them up. In the small statue of Nefertiti, for instance, the hands are drawn down, and, seen from the front, they seem completely detached from their stone matrix. But, seen from the side, instead of leaning back against the stone pillar, the body hangs in a sinuous arabesque against the vertical line of the support. Yet the work has been executed with such skill that we ignore its limitations. Despite the attitude there is no stiffness in the tired body with its slightly lax shapes, its narrow drooping shoulders, its breadth of hips and stomach, which remind us of the nudes of the Bruges school. Despite the somewhat cruel veracity of details, the work maintains a discreet restraint which must have been strengthened by the painted-on clothing.

Among the technical innovations belonging to Amarna art we must note a method used by sculptors in addition to low relief and work in the round: the incrustation of coloured stones to give more life to reliefs meant to be viewed in the strong light that bathed the courts of the temples and of the official palace. In this curious technique, which was later used only in the minor arts, the sculptors of Amarna attained a remark,able mastery. They employed it on work in the round: on a body cut from the crystal limestone peculiar to the Amarna region, which reproduced the white linen robe—the head and limbs being added. These latter were fashioned in a material that suggested naked flesh: yellow or red jasper, according as to whether the subject was queen or king, and yet oftener in the quartz sandstone in which the warm colour imitated sun, browned skin marvellously well. Here lies the explanation of the many heads with the skull cut level and supplied with tenons for the support of head,dress or crown of some other material. The necks were made unnaturally long so that they could be inserted in a limestone body.

These composite statues, which do not harmonize with our aesthetic values, were certainly put together by different sculptors, as an odd text by Diodoros verifies.[16] Perhaps the various parts were collected at a definite place. Such a method would have simplified the question of transport and would explain why in certain studios, as in Tuthmosis', nothing else but heads at different stages of completion have been found.

The use of hard stone called for a different technique than that we have been con, sidering in works of softer materials. Granite or sandstone, which lacks lustre, required a treatment unlike that of limestone with its naturally luminous quality. Colour is absent and the sculptor must capture the play of light and shadow if his modelling is to be effective. Now for the first time, it seems, stones were sought for—primarily in terms of their inherent qualities: a close texture, fine shades of colour, and above all a greater or less luminosity in the material, influence the new sculptural style.

The samples of various stones found in Tuthmosis' studio prove by themselves the new interest given to the choice of materials; but it is in the products that we appreciate the success of the experiments. Formerly, when granite was too speckled and spoiled the delicacy of modelling, the pieces were often painted in several colours; the hard stone was chosen for its strength, not its appearance. In Amarna, on the contrary, we find heads sculptured in a brownish sandstone which strongly suggests the warm tones of the skin and which the sculptor knew how to take advantage of, while subtly stressing eye, lids and lips with a brush.

This quest for the effects that can be drawn from hard stone is revealed by a kind of modelling devised solely to catch the light. Among the many effigies of Nefertiti, the small one in orange sandstone, found in Tuthmosis's studio, is one of the most striking examples of the new approach. If we compare it with the polychrome bust of the queen, we recognize that despite deviations in detail they are really close to one another. The sandstone head is unfinished and the large ears disfigure it when frontally viewed. The very simple modelling shows none of the bust's emaciations; the eyelids, shorter than in the bust, throw a slight shadow on the eyes, which are faintly outlined by a touch of colour; the delicate curves of the mouth are brought to life by a pale rose tint. The same method appears in a head still in its preliminary stages, where the rather dull material (a grey granite) takes on under the light makeup a more stricken and violent expression. The habit of colouring unfinished heads so as to judge in advance what they will look like, becomes a studio-trick which can be forgiven because of the discretion with which the sculptors used it.

Beyond doubt the most beautiful in the series of heads is that in Cairo Museum. If we compare it with the other portraits of the queen, we note some differences, but they have nothing to do with the model's features. Rather, they represent shades of interpretation and style, which demonstrate conclusively that the sculptors of Amarna have, despite everything, stamped their works with a personal vision. We have already stressed that they did not work from the living model; they did not have to seize the mobility and the complexity which a sitter always presents; they did not need to be concerned with reproducing the fugitive expression which changes the features. Not being subjected to the model's involuntary influence, they did not fall into the easy snare of seeking a mere resemblance. The mask or plaster-model served as a sort of 'developer' by bringing out, better than the actual face could, the essential forms which the artist then transposed into the chosen material. A close examination of the Cairo head reveals the successive stages of its execution. While the back of the head still shows the marks of the bronze point (these would have been hidden under a head-dress made from some other stone), the face has already undergone the process of *abrasion* which was used to remove all traces of the chisel. This polishing with emery powder took a very long time, and the perfection and beauty of the stone depended on it. Photography shows clearly the different phases. Work was held up just as the sculptor was beginning to deal with the particularly fine modelling of the nostrils, the periphery of the eyes and the lips with their warming tint of rose. To make sure of his points of guidance and to obviate errors, he used a brush to draw a median line of dividing the face in its length, and to stress the eyes, brows, mouth and the edge of the head-dress. The successive phases of execution are thus linked in a steady concentration of all the elements composing the work. We catch that work in the midst of its process of gestation, and yet it already imposes itself on us though the life in it has not yet matured. How strange and moving is this mysterious quality which subsists in works of art far removed from us in time and which suddenly brings them so close. Does not the beautiful Nefertiti of Cairo possess the same discreet modesty, the same tenderness, as Despiau's women?

Among the many heads of princesses discovered at Amarna, those with curiously elongated skulls have aroused a large number of controversies. We can at once discard the theory of artificially deformed skulls. This characteristic has never been noted by Dr Derry who has examined several thousand Egyptian skulls of all periods.[17] A second suggestion has been made that this peculiar skull-formation represents a head-dress. But the Amarna sculptors have always clearly indicated details of clothing; and their concern with such matters often led them, as we saw, to leave the top of the head with a simple tenon, so that a head-dress in some other material might be later fixed on. If we examine the fragment of painting, now in the Ashmolean Museum at Oxford, which shows two of the princesses seated at their mother's feet, we find that their distorted heads own a few straight hairs; there is no sign at all of a head-dress. According to Dr Derry's studies of the mummies of Tutankhamen and Amenkhkere, it seems however, that members of the royal family had a tendency to the 'platycephalic' type. In the princesses this tendency might have been accentuated by their maternal ancestry. E. Meyer tells us that the Mitannians had a 'dolichocephalic and elongated skull, flattened at the back and slightly indented towards the middle'.[18] Now, these are precisely the characteristics we see plainly in the heads of the princesses, especially in that of the most beautiful of them, whom we can take as example for the others. The peculiarities were then natural, but they have been deliberately exaggerated when transposed into the work of art.

We are thus confronted with a plastic deformation that derived from a conscious aesthetic and became fashionable. All the people of Amarna wanted to be represented in this way, and we continue to find a reflection of the curious tendency in reliefs of the Ramessid period.

The strange heads of the princesses are quite in line with the colossi of Karnak, but the brutality of the latter has been modified into a new mannerism. Under the almost caricatural ugliness of the faces, under the deliberate lack of expression, we feel a dynamic tension seething. The crystalline sandstone lends itself admirably to the stylization of these heads in which the formal expressionism reminds us to some extent of the mystery-charged hieratic quality of certain African carvings. A great expressive force emanates from these works, though the effect is so studied and the charm so reticent that we need a moment's consideration before being carried away. We have to disregard the physical deformity and contemplate only the expert construction, the *cosa mentale* which the artist has conceived. The meticulous and powerful modelling that envelops the volumes has no break to the eye or the touch; it is the same in nature as the linear scheme enclosing the bodies in the reliefs. In the reliefs indeed expressionism went farthest and was longest maintained. The workers of the necropolis, isolated like pariahs, probably did not work from the same documents as the sculptors. Instead of the 'return to nature' desired by their sovereign, their art was often held fast in a formal language derived from the techniques they used. The king's outline remained the point of departure for new forms, but to estimate those forms at their true value, we must look on them, not as 'images' of the royal family, but as a sort of decorative vegetation, an arabesque which expressed by its undulant and rhythmic grace the fragile reverie ominous of approaching doom. The reliefs are not then the place in which to seek the 'human appearance' of the king and queen. Rather we must turn to the studios and above all to that of 'the Chief Sculptor Tuthmosis.' But there also two aesthetic conceptions are found to clash: an expressionist style that tends towards abstraction in its extreme manifestations, and a conformism revived in works almost insipid through their excess of sweetness and suavity.

The art of the Amarna revolution had started off with a shattering break from tradition; after some years it reverted to a more harmonious conception of the human image. Still, it was not really a return to the ideal of the previous reign. The sculptors of Amarna had created works of a personal style by fusing two new factors: the choice of materials for their intrinsic qualities and the use of light-effects. The close texture of stone, its colour, its greater or less luminosity, became important elements in the creation of a work of art. For the first time, also, sculptors took account of the role of light in the ordering and density of volumes. By the contrasts of shadow and brightness it strengthened the clarity of outlines, it enriched subtle passages, it enveloped motionless forms with a grave and serene elegance. Thanks to its illumination, modelling became more than a means of representation; it turned into a means of expression and soon into a new mannerism.

By consciously accepting the part played by light in the working out of their products, the sculptors of Amarna managed to set the latter forever in the same space as that of the spectator. In so doing, they introduced one of the essential ingredients of sculpture in all periods.

*IX  Princesses at the feet of their parents*

X  *Bust of Queen Nefertiti*

*XI  The same in profile*

XII  *Painted floor from the Great Palace*

# 5. THE DEATH OF AKHENATEN AND THE END OF THE AMARNA ADVENTURE

No sooner had Akhenaten and his family definitely settled down in Amarna than news reached the Egyptian court of a palace-revolution in which Tushratta, King of Mitanni and father-in-law of the Pharaoh, had been murdered. Taking advantage of confusion in the capital and of the flight of Mattiwasa, the dead man's son, to the Babylonian court, Artatama II of Hurri (brother or cousin of Tushratta), with the aid of the Assyrian king, invaded Mitanni. On the still vacant throne he installed his own son Sutarna. Assuruballit, in reward for his aid, was made Protector of Mitanni and in his turn assumed the title of Great King—to the resentful fury of his neighbour Burra-buriash, who still considered the Assyrians as his vassals. Rather than intervene in the conflict, the Hittite King Suppuluiumas chose to consolidate his positions in northern Syria, where he was to be kept occupied during the greater part of Akhenaten's reign. As we shall see later, his long patience was to get its recompense.[1]

Preoccupied with the anxieties and labours of their adventure, the Pharaoh and his disciples do not seem to have grasped the gravity of the events in the Near East, where Tushratta's death was a fresh portent. To replace the Mitannian alliance, which had made possible the long era of peace in the previous reign, Akhenaten held fast to the same policy as his father and preferred reconciliation to armed intervention. He embarked on negotiations with Burraburiash with a view to marriage with one of his daughters. The letters exchanged up to this point with the oriental monarch show that the Pharaoh did not spare his correspondent's feelings. The latter on several occasions complained that the King of Egypt had failed to acknowledge the congratulations sent to him at the time of his accession and had never shown the least interest in his [Burraburiash's] precarious health. In his last letter he demanded compensation for the plundering of his caravans in Canaan where the Egyptian police were supposed to be responsible for maintaining order. It was high time, then, to placate him by asking for the hand of one of his daughters. The Egyptian envoy (was it Ay?) arrived in Babylon escorted by three thousand warriors and bearing many gifts in gold (or gold plate) of which the potentate had need. He was informed that the promised girl had died but that another princess was ready to set out for Egypt, accompanied by a governess of Egyptian origin. The luxurious trousseau, of which the list still exists, included numerous jewels; one neck-lace was composed of 'a thousand and forty-eight precious stones'. The princess, it seems, was to become the mother of the young Tutankhamen, who must have been born about the seventh year, since he was about ten years old on his accession.

In the eighth year, during an inspection of his domain, Akhenaten again confirmed the oath he had taken in the sixth year, and an inscription to that effect was duly added in correct form to the boundary stelae set up two years before.

Next year a change appeared in the titulary of the god Aten. The names of Horus-the-Falcon and Shu, god of the air, which had been used, were now suppressed. New titles were enclosed in cartouches, as with royal names. Henceforth Aten was to be '(the Living Rē, Lord of the Horizon, who trembles joyously on the Horizon) (in his Name "Rē the Father who has come back as Aten".)'[2] At the same time, in view of the ceremony of the Divine Jubilee, the god also was given the title of Lord of the Jubilee. On the stelae and in tomb-inscriptions the divine name in its cartouche took precedence of the king's; Aten was henceforth considered as the ruler and the king became his co-regent. The linking of the divine name with that of the venerable Rē, the title of Chief Seer for his high priest, the presence of the sacred bull Mnevis, are so many concessions towards the clergy of Heliopolis, whose support the king was seeking. The march of the religious reform began to mark time; the new faith, tainted for many with heresy, scarcely extended past the domain of Amarna. By stressing once again that Aten was an emanation of 'Rē the Father', the king officially declared his orthodoxy. He set out his position further by naming his last two daughters by the queen Nefer-neferu-Rē (Beauty of Rē's Beauties) and Setep-en-Re (Re's Chosen). But the first girl had hardly been weaned when a great misfortune struck the family: the death of little Makitaten, the second daughter of the rulers. The king, whose affection for his children showed on every occasion, must have felt a profound grief. It may have been from this moment that his health, already fragile, became gravely undermined. We have practically no precise information about this dramatic event; only the scenes on the royal tomb bring us an echo of it.

Let us imagine the sculptor Tuthmosis called to the bedside of the dead child to mould her deathmask. Sunken by disease, the worn features were hardly recognizable under the heavy royal head-band that weighed upon them. We would like to believe that on his return to the studio the sculptor at once set about recording in stone the gentle childish face imprinted on his memory. His chisel's touch was as light as a caress, and the eyelids with their veiled expression preserved that 'moist gleam' to which the poet Lucan later referred when speaking of Praxiteles's work.

The most important historical event of the Amarna period, of which we possess a precise date and a description, is the visit made in the twelfth year by the Queen-mother Tiy and her suite.[3] It is more than likely that this intelligent and realistically-minded woman, owning a thorough experience of state-affairs, had never approved of the intransigent measures of her son against Amun's party or the harsh and irreversible break of the sixth year. Even if she had once favoured the cult of Aten, the purified form of which was better suited to the ideals of her cosmopolitan entourage, and if as well she had encouraged the views of her brother Aaen, Great Seer of Rē and rival of the Theban god's First Prophet, she was far too shrewd to enter into an open conflict with the Amarna powers. If her son had not been a visionary, who had lost his sense of realities, some compromise might have been arranged. Religious toleration, natural for Egyptians, would have accepted the presence of the two gods side by side.

Left alone, or almost alone, in the great Theban palace, Tiy had all the time needed for meditating on Egypt's misfortunes. Sometimes a courier brought her a message from Akhetaten, where she still could count on some faithful friends among those of her own generation. Among these were Panehesi, chancellor of the North, who kept in a corner of his house a stele set up in memory of his former master, King Amenophis III; Ramose, once steward of that dead king; or indeed her own brother Ay—though she considered him largely responsible for the indoctrination of the Pharaoh. She no longer received news from Asia since the death of her old friend Tushratta; but disturbing rumours were carried to her by some Egyptian official or other bringing his family home because of the growing insecurity of the Syrian towns. In Egypt, too, the situation was daily deteriorating. Thebes had lost its rank of capital and become a provincial town, badly kept and given over to disorder. The deserted temples and palaces were breaking up and grass grew in the courtyards. After sunset the roads were no longer safe; brigands roamed about and held travellers to ransom; the royal tombs, it was rumoured, were being violated and pillaged without action from the police whose wages were not paid.[4] Counter-measures were urgently needed. Was Tiy the first person to urge them? Did she send an envoy to Akhenaten to try out his reactions? Huia, her faithful chamberlain, seems to have played an important part on this occasion; he may have served as a go-between and organized the meeting.

An official pretext for the reunion of mother and son was easily found in the inauguration of a small sanctuary, 'the Shadow of Rē', which was to be dedicated to the queen-mother and the dead king.[5] A building of this sort had already been dedicated to Queen Nefertiti; and excavators have found another at Maruaten, which had been dedicated to Princess Maritaten and probably built at the time of her wedding. The Shadow-of-Rē was composed of a series of pillared courts, between which stood statues of Tiy. Amenophis III, and Akhenaten. Its site was probably on the riverbank to the south of the great Palace, but the encroachment of tillage has made it impossible to be sure of the exact place.

The presence there of statues of Amenophis III explains the use of the mask and the model of the dead king found in the studio of Tuthmosis. The sculptor was probably commissioned to execute the heads of the king, which were all identical, intended for the numerous statues ornamenting the temple.

During her stay at Akhetaten the queen-mother doubtless had discussions with her son about the political situation. The local lords of Syria and Palestine, remaining true to Egypt, kept on sending more and more alarming messages. Instead of hurrying to their aid, Akhenaten preferred to listen to the insinuations of a certain Aziru, son of Abdi-Asirta prince of Amurru. We have already noted this man in intrigues with the Hittite King. On his arrival at the Egyptian court, he managed to slip into the good graces of Tutu, minister of foreign affairs, and protested his loyalty. In the midst of all this, news of Abdi-Asirta's assassination came; and Aziru, obtaining the post of governing Amurru from the king, returned to Syria. While still assuring the Pharaoh of his fidelity, he soon went over to the Hittites and seized the Phoenician ports to the north of Byblos. Meanwhile, the lord of Byblos, Rib-Addi, was warning the Pharaoh against the conduct of Aziru; he painted the situation in dark tones and added, 'When I used to write to your Father, he hearkened to my words and sent archers . . . Since your Father went away from Sidon, the country has fallen into the hand of the Habiru.' 'Why does the King my Lord write to me: "Protect yourself and you will be protected"?'—or as we would say today, 'God helps those who help themselves'.

For his part, Burraburiash, seeing his old vassal Assyria raising its head again, was perturbed in turn. He sent messages to the king, saying, that if he did not take urgent measures to reassert his authority he would lose the whole land of Canaan.

Tiy must have added her exhortations to those of Egypt's remaining allies, and Akhenaten at last acted. He ordered his general Bikhuru, stationed in Syria, to investigate things. The general carried out his instructions so blunderingly that he may justly be suspected of having taken bribes from Aziru. He attacked Rib-Addi and played into the hands of his country's enemies. Driven out of his own town, the unfortunate Rib-Addi ended by being murdered and Azuri seized Byblos. The town of Simyra, which had remained faithful, received no aid and soon also was captured.

When news of the fall of Byblos and Simyra reached the Egyptian court, it must have come as a sad shock. Urged by his mother, the king wrote an angry letter to Aziru, reproaching him for not 'having always told the truth', and ordering him to come and explain his actions—otherwise the Pharaoh would come in person and chastise him. Aziru disregarded the letter. An army under command of general Iankhamu then received orders to regain Simyra.

This ephemeral victory was doubtless the occasion of the great ceremony for the reception of foreign tributes, which was earlier mentioned: a final piece of propaganda to throw dust in the eyes of the Egyptians and reassure them that everything was as well as could be in the best of worlds.

Within a few weeks Akhetaten was to reach its apogee.

A feverish activity took hold of the capital where teams of workers laboured in successive shifts to finish the constructions on time. In the great Temple they busied themselves at erecting the pavilion to be used in the tribute-ceremony, and which was set on the wall of the temenos overlooking the wadi. Invitations were sent out by special couriers, requesting the presence of all notables from north and south Egypt. Their apartments were made ready; lodgings and stables were whitewashed afresh for the troops that would arrive from Memphis with General Horemheb. Everywhere houses were repaired, gardens raked clean, courts repaved. Every day from the left bank the feluccas brought sacks of grain, preserves of dried fish, jars of oil, big garlands of onions, lowing cattle, frightened goat-kids, noisy ducks and geese. Big amphoras of wine and beer were carefully laid down in the cool cellars.

The craftsmen, too, were as active. Potters spread rows of pots and bowls out in the sun before firing them. The Mycenean pastry-maker, as a shrewd businessman, ground

71 *Bust of Princess Makitaten ( ? )*

72  *Small head of the Princess Makitaten ( ? )*　　　　　73  *Death-mask of the Princess Makitaten ( ? )*

74 *Musicians*

75 Top: *Two princesses*

76 Bottom: *Dancers and singers*

77 Top: *Head of King Smenkhkare (?)*

78 Bottom: *The Princess Ankhesenpaaten brings an offering of bread to the god Aten*

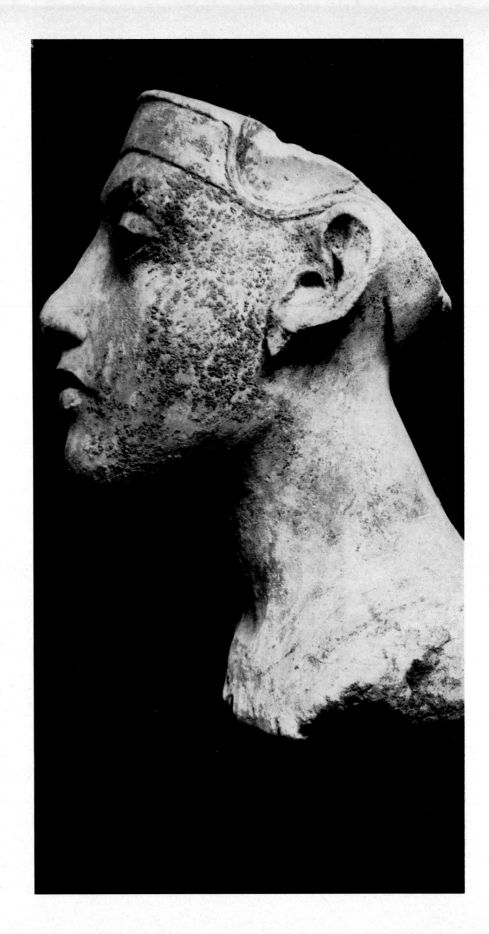

79  *Smenkhkare ( ? )*

80  *Smenkhkare ( ? ). Sculptor's model*

81  *King Akhenaten and Smenkhkare dining. Private stele*

82  *Unfinished stele. King Akhenaten and Smenkhkare dining*

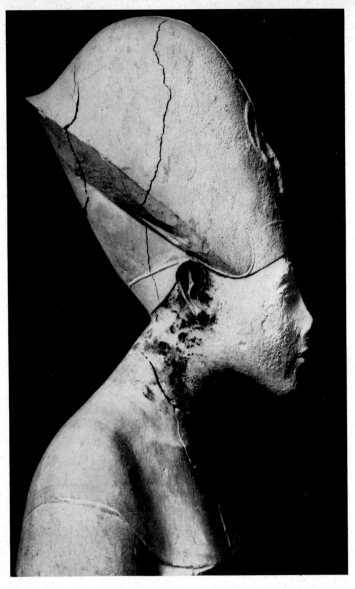

*83  Seated portrait of Smenkhkare ( ? )*

*84  Bust of King Akhenaten*

85  *Unfinished group: Akhenaten with a princess on his knee*

86 *Asiatic prisoners; from the tomb of Horemheb*
87 Below: *Negro prisoners, from the tomb of Horemheb*
88 Top right: *Nubian princesses and attendants*
89 Bottom right: *A horseman*

90 *King Ay as the Nile God*

fine flour and stored up honey for the great day when his freshly whitened shop would swarm with customers.

Great ladies and middle-class wives hustled their servant-girls about and badgered the weavers for their new tunics. Wig-makers were busy. Shoemakers cut sandals all day from the tanned skins hanging on the workshop walls. Jewellers were also rushed off their feet; they had to reset the sumptuous necklaces and repair diadems and bracelets brought up from the bottom of jewel-boxes. Some grandmothers in a mood of generosity gave their jewels to delighted granddaughters while recalling great occasions of the past when they themselves had worn them.

On the great day, early in the morning, before the noon-heat, the entire royal family mustered and left the palace in their palanquins between two rows of ambassadors and high dignitaries all bending their knees. At the entrance to the great Temple, the priests prostrated themselves with their skulls shining in the sun; slaves shook tinkling sistra; harps and lutes sounded; incense rose up spiralling from the hundreds of altars loaded with offerings and flowers. At the moment when the royal procession entered the court-yard, choirs struck up the triumphal hymn to Aten.

The pavilion of tributes reared up glittering against the sky, its banners floating in the breeze. One after the other, the bearers lowered their palanquins and the rulers went into the edifice, followed by the officiating priests, and each withdrew to a separate room to carry out the ritual ablutions indispensable before every ceremony of a religious character.

After being clad in consecrated robes, the Pharaoh and his retinue proceeded towards the tribute which dominated the vast plain that glistened in the blinding light. Every-where, along the wadi's banks, an immense crowd was packed, held back with diffi-culty by the Mazoi of Commandant Mahu. When Akhenaten appeared, the cheering broke out: 'Life! Prosperity! Health!' The sovereign replied to the ovations by raising his hand. Three of the princesses were present: the eldest, Meritaten, had just passed her twelfth birthday. She was already a young girl, matured by grief, while her sisters still kept the frolicsomeness of childhood. All three of them discreetly observed a hand-some young man who had come from Thebes with their grandmother. They had been told that he was their uncle Smenkhkere. Slim and elegant, he stood near their aunt Bakitaten and their great uncle Ay, who had the sullen air of his bad days.

Suddenly a great silence fell. Everyone turned towards the east, where something was happening on the horizon. One after another, the hills of rosy sand were covered by a moving host out of which shone the momentary gleams of polished weapons. Soon the spectators could distinguish the chariots of the cavalry drawn by white stallions from Babylon. The young officers driving them were clad in battle-tunics and armed with bows; their ornamented quivers were fixed to the chariot frames. The first chariot was that of the commander-in-chief, Horemheb, who stood impassive at his driver's side; he wore many gold collars and gloves of red leather which the Pharaoh had given him. As he passed before the tribune, he raised his arm in salute. After the chariots came the swift archers, bow in hand and sandals attached to their left shoulders. Then the infantry with their big leather shields and heavy bronze javelins. Following the army appeared a shining troop of bearded men with long curly hair, clad in variegated robes. Some held the bridle of stallions which, made nervous by the cries and the movement, threw the procession into a slight disorder. Others bore arms decorated with gold and lapis lazuli, swords and daggers of iron—that very rare metal. Porters were bent double under the weight of vessels of wrought silver or stone vases full of valuable oils. Syrian slaves, their arms loaded with embroidered stuffs, closed the march. Then a second procession came in sight. Now it was one of Nubians, and their arrival revived the general curiosity. They were bringing a profusion of panther and leopard skins, enormous elephant tusks, gold ingots, and sometimes strange animals held in leash by black slaves. The great motley crowd halted and prostrated itself before the royal tribune. Servants of the Temple rushed forward, gathered up the gifts, and went to arrange them in the wings of the pavilion or in the inner court, while the exotic animals were led off to adorn the cages of the zoological garden.

As the procession ended, the onlookers dispersed towards the suburbs, talking about the spectacle. The king, before returning to the Palace, went to bless the tributes that were going to replenish once more the Temple reserves to the great relief of Panehesi, superintendent of Aten's stores. Already the scribes had their writing-cases in their hands; they were making an inventory and setting down lists on papyrus rolls.

In the evening of this memorable day a great feast was held in the royal Palace. Huia described it in a lively manner, and we have already mentioned it. After the banquet, musicians and dancers won prolonged applause from the guests, to whom young slaves brought fruit and flowers. In the town, singing and carousal came to an end only with the dawn. The festivities were over, with all the illusory pageant that did nothing to hide from clear-seeing eyes the grave problems of the moment.

Taking advantage of the presence of the ambassadors, the army chiefs, and the heads of the administration in Amarna, Queen Tiy did not fail to inquire into the attitude of people in the other parts of the country. Foreign envoys confirmed the dangerous position in the Asian provinces; others described the army's unrest, the discontent of the civil service, and the growing opposition of those who had been dispossessed by the regime and whose hopes were now reviving. And so, the last sounds of revelry were hardly over and the last farewells pronounced, when the queen-mother called upon her son. The time had come to speak of the royal succession, a problem which was much on her mind. In the event of an accident the Pharaoh had no male heir old enough to succeed him; and his health was far from being first-rate, added Tiy, examining with a worried look her son's drawn face, his thin bent shoulders and swollen stomach. Knowing his obstinacy, she was cautious about the way in which she spoke of her plan. The eldest princess was just twelve years old; the time for marrying her had come. The queen-mother had a fully eligible candidate to propose: Smenkhkere, Akhenaten's half-brother. He was eighteen years old, a king's son; in marrying him Meritaten would preserve the purity of solar blood for the dynasty. In a few years he could participate in the government and thus assure the succession of power.

What she omitted to say was that he had spent his childhood in Thebes and had never, in the eyes of the Amunians, been implicated in what they called 'the heresy'. In the person of Smenkhkere a reconciliation would one day become possible; and Tiy, with her lucid mind, had grown convinced since her arrival in Akhetaten that this solution could ensure the dynasty's future.

She took account of the fact that the king would never break his oath and that he would never agree to recognize his defeat by returning to Thebes. Patience was needed. Time and the gods would bring the solution about, Tiy told herself; with age she had acquired a good dose of traditional Egyptian wisdom.

Since her visit she had noticed the strong influence which her daughter-in-law Nefertiti had established over the king. Nefertiti was intelligent and cultured; her un-failing beauty had kept her husband's affection intact; but what was obstinacy in him was in her absolute intransigence. Her faith was fanatical; she sustained the Pharaoh's religious fervour without allowing the least falling-away. She had been meant on her arrival in Egypt for the royal harem; but Akhenaten's love had set her on the throne. Remembering her own experience, Tiy could understand how the proud Nefertiti had suffered from the Theban aristocracy's disdain. By encouraging the king to break with the established order, she had taken her revenge for certain humiliations. Tiy recalled disagreements which had set them in opposition to one another, and how she had been embittered by her daughter-in-law's victory. For the rest she would have to allow for a lack of enthusiasm on Nefertiti's part for the project of uniting her daughter with a suitor not of her own choice. So Tiy considered that she would lose no time; the marriage had better take place while she herself was still staying in the capital.

To gain her son's consent she summoned Ay. She had never trusted him. In marry-ing Nefertiti's nurse he had thrown himself heart and soul into the queen's cause. The doctrinaire of the revolution, he had found in Nefertiti a docile disciple, who at the same time was an ardent partisan. When she translated for him the chants of her people, she had transmitted to him the poetic metaphors which were often to inspire him as he composed the solar hymns with the king. Tiy could not hope to find an ally in her brother. Even if he looked favourably on Meritaten's marriage, he would never accept the least turning-back on the chosen path.

Was Smenkhkere the child of the incestuous union of Amenophis III and his daughter Satamun? or was he son of the Babylonian princess who came to Egypt about the same time? An examination of his mummy reveals that he was between twenty-three and twenty-five at the time of his death in the seventeenth year of Akhenaten's reign.[6] Thus he was born about the twenty-ninth year of the previous reign. We have noted earlier the probable reason for Amenophis's marriage with his own daughter. At the time of Smenkhkere's birth Queen Tiy was at least 40 years old, if not more. She had had several daughters, and the birth of the last one, Bakitaten, had removed all hopes of her producing more children. Smenkhkere was the son of Satamun and thus was also Tiy's grandson. That family tie would explain the presence of his remains in her tomb.[7] That he was Amenophis's son is certain; for he had the hereditary defect of protruding incisors characteristic of all the Pharaohs of this dynasty. What differentiated him from the paternal line were certain Indo-European features which we find among the Mitan-nians, the Hurrians, and the Kassites of ancient Asia. He could have inherited them from his great-grandfather Muia (if he were Satamun's son) or from the Babylonian princess. His cephalic index is almost identical with that of Tutankhamen, his future brother-in-law, successor, and nephew. The breadths of the two skulls exceed those of normal Egyptian skulls. Akhenaten's mummy has not been found; but we may assume that, like his daughters, he had the 'platycephalic' skull explicable by the foreign or the consanguineous marriages. The royal portraits show us the great resemblance between Akhenaten and his sons-in-law, which is further evidence of their close family relationship.

The marriage of Meritaten and Smenkhkere took place soon afterwards, and we may guess that it was the occasion for many festivities. Before long the young prince was named as co-regent. Queen Tiy could return to Thebes, well content.

On the occasion of Smenkhkere's enthronement a vast reception-hall was built at the southern end of the great Palace. Meritaten received a 'Shadow of Rē', which her father had constructed as a gift in the middle of a large stretch of water in Maruaten's estate. The marriage consoled the king for the death of his second daughter Makitaten and restored his confidence in the future. He took such a strong liking to his son-in-law that they were to be seen together at all hours of the day. Out of jealousy the queen refused to appear in public and rumours went round of discord between the pair that had once been so lovingly united. The sculptors in their often naive way expressed the new royal infatuation by replacing the queen's silhouette, on the small stelae for domestic use, with that of the co-regent turned affectionately towards the king or offering him a drink. The situation went from bad to worse till one day Nefertiti took her children and left the royal villa. Because of her royal oath to the god, she could not remove from Akhetaten; but she withdrew to the north of the area. There she had a new palace built, which she named Hat-Aten, Aten's Castle. The old Hat-Aten which she had vacated, she was saying in effect, no longer existed in her eyes. The king retaliated by giving his son-in-law the name with which he had once endowed his beloved queen; he called Smenkhkere Nefer-neferu-Aten (Beauty of Aten's Beauties). On monuments the cartouche of the young princes gradually replaced that of the queen. The artists were busy reproducing the features of the co-regent; his effigies multiplied in the artists' studios like the charming reliefs specially made for sentimental souls in which we see the princess offering her young husband mandragores, fruit symbolizing love, while he leans nonchalantly on a staff.

Separated from the queen and perhaps from Ay, Akhenaten doubtless lent a more attentive ear to overtures coming from Thebes. We may conjecture that Tiy on her return took part in the preliminary negotiations and encouraged the idea of a delegation to Akhenaten. Smenkhkere, who was bound by no oath to Aten and had never been compromised in the religious disputes, could well be used as a peace-envoy. It is not impossible indeed that he went first to Memphis to attempt a reconciliation with Ptah's clergy; for a quartz head, found in the temple's ruins, seems clearly to represent his features. Another head, suggesting rather Akhenaten, was discovered in the same place. the two fragments might have come from an offering made in common by the two kings to the gods.

A graffito in the tomb of a certain Pairi at Thebes mentions the building of a palace and the consecration of a monument to Amun by the co-regent in the third year of his reign.[8] We have no further information about this offering; but perhaps we can

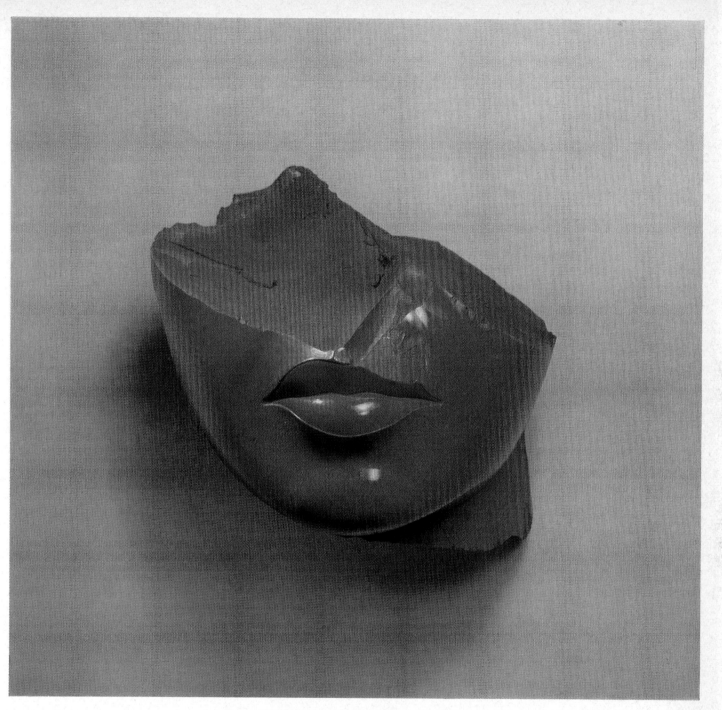

*XIII  Fragment of a head of Queen Tiy ( ? )*

XIV  Left: *Head of a princess (Ankhesenpaaten ?)*
XV  *The Pharaoh Smenkhkare ( ? ) (profile)*

*XVI  Smenkhkare and Meritaten walking in a garden*

recognize it in a celebrated group in steatite in the Louvre Museum, of which only the figure of the king seated on the throne survives. Here would then be the first product of the Theban 'Restoration', which still retains, though in an attenuated way, something of the Amarna style.

The decisive step had been taken without the Pharaoh, who had remained in Amarna, needing to make apologies or lose face in the eyes of his subjects. Queen Tiy could congratulate herself on success in her aims, and could believe that the reconcilia-tion was going to be definite. Unfortunately, the premature death of Smenkhkere quite wrecked the whole enterprise and everything was once again unsettled. We know no details of his death; but it is evident that the young co-regent suffered from the same troubles as the other members of the family, the result of an acute degeneracy which made them all extremely frail.

He was buried at Thebes in the Valley of Kings, in a tomb without epigraph. It had perhaps been meant for Queen Tiy, as her jewels and part of her funerary furniture were found there. On the other hand, Princess Meritaten lived to a ripe old age and seems to have died under Horemheb.[9]

After the departure of Smenkhkere and Meritaten for Thebes (where she was styled Meritamun), Akhenaten had only two more years to live. We do not know if his death preceded or followed Smenkhkere's. If he died after his son-in-law, we could find some explanation of the incredible event which seems to have occurred about this time. Smenkhkere had had no issue and his death had again left the throne without a succes-sor. When Akhenaten died, his third daughter Ankhenspaaten was at the most thirteen years old; her half-brother Tutankhamen to whom she was betrothed was scarcely ten years. Though she was nubile, he was still a child, and in any case only a concubine's son. Did Akhenaten, feeling the shadow of death, hope to preserve his line by marrying his own daughter, as his father had previously done? He considered himself the 'beloved Son of God, born of his flesh': in his eyes the marriage was a theogamy, a sacred act. That is the sole justification we can offer for the macabre union of a dying man and an adolescent girl, the fruit of which bore the same name as the girl's mother.[10]

We are equally ignorant of the circumstances of the Pharaoh's death, though we can imagine that his lonely end was profoundly sad. Did he die in the apartments of his own Hat-Aten, in the room where the walls still bore in vivid colours the image of his family happiness? We should like to think Nefertiti forgot their quarrels and, faithful to the name given her by the king in their old days, returned to close his eyes.

He was buried in the tomb which he had had dug out in the Dark-el-Melk and to which the Princess Makitaten had preceded him a few years before. The burial place was probably tracked down and violated, and the mummy destroyed, at the time of the Amunian reaction. It was 'officially' discovered again only in 1892; but the inhabitants of the region seem to have known of its location, as objects from it found in their posses-sion before that date would tend to prove.[11]

The king's death coming so soon after that of the co-regent left the throne to a child. We know nothing of the first regnal years of the young Tutankhaten. They doubtless passed careless and happy, in the royal harem, in the shade of fragrant gardens, amid thickets of acacias and sycamores, close to flowering ponds, with thousands of many coloured birds hidden along the luxuriant banks. Possibly Akhenaten used to come there to find rest at times from his official duties and to watch with absent-minded glance the boy's play. Then one day his death deprived the child of this innocent happiness and suddenly burdened him with a heavy heritage. The boy became king and married his half-sister, Ankhesenpaaten, whom he had hardly ever seen. Henceforth he spent his time with the child-queen and her sisters, except when he was drawn away by official ceremonies or by the sports and exercises proper to a youth who must be able to throw the boomerang, shoot arrows, and drive a light chariot fearlessly at the full gallop of two Babylonian stallions. And there were also hours for study when the Divine Father Ay taught the young king the holy doctrine and the way to behave before the god's altar.

The young couple lived with Queen Nefertiti in Aten's Castle. She still had enough supporters to enable her to regain control of the situation with the aid of Ay, now named as vizier. Life for the young folk was an unceasing festival, but the queen-mother and her counsellors, Ay and his wife Ty, regarded the future with disquet. For some years Nefertiti's intransigence triumphed and succeeded in maintaining the heretical faith despite the increasing defections of those who considered it a lost cause.

While Egypt was rent by factions, foreign tribute was no longer sent, and diplomatic and commercial relations were disrupted. The tidings of the capture of Carchemish by the Hittite king sounded the deathknell of the Egyptians in Asia. This victory, which coincided with the accession of Tutankhaten, permitted the Hittites to make them-selves masters of the whole of the north of the Near East. In Canaan the city lords deserted the Pharaoh's cause and surrendered to new invaders, the Habiru, while the last Palestinians who remained loyal fell heroically before the gates of Zilu on the Egyptian frontier. The revolt of Canaan had severed relations between the Nile Valley and Babylonia; Burraburiash accepted an alliance with his old vassal, Assyria, and married its king's daughter. No longer feeling safe in Babylon after this conjunction, Tushratta's son took refuge at the Hittite court, where he was welcomed with open arms. Suppiluliumas gave him his daughter for wife and promised to aid him on the first favourable occasion to reconquer his kingdom. Soon the raids of Phoenician pirates grew so common as to interrupt sea communications. The cities of Syria and Palestine, once flourishing, fell one after the other before the penetration of Semitic tribes and the growing menace of the power of the Hittites and their allies the Armenians.

In half a century the magnificent conquests of the Tuthmosid Pharaohs had crum-bled to nothing as a result of their descendants' indifference and negligence in foreign affairs. Egypt, however, was not completely ousted from her provinces. Under-Tutank-haten occurred a sharp reawakening of the national consciousness when General Horemheb was entrusted with the mission of reconquering southern Palestine. He set out his victories on the walls of his fine Memphite tomb, where we see Asians humbly advancing towards him to do homage and beg for the right of asylum.

Probably the death of Queen Nefertiti was what brought about the end of Atenian resistance. The heresy's last champion, she remained true to her oath to the very end. Her death allowed Ay, always an opportunist, to resume negotiations with the victorious followers of Amun and thus to save the dynasty. We can imagine the violent arguments, the haggling, which took place till Amun had won the day and the return of the young king to Thebes was decided upon. Henceforth he was called Tutankhamen (the Living Statue of Amun) and his young queen was called Ankhesenamun (She who lives by Amun).

It is easy to imagine the young royal couple at Thebes, easy victims in the intrigues woven round the throne. The king's first obligation had to be to restore the monuments and the official cult of Amun. A stele found at Karnak describes these undertakings and also the great hardships of the times, when all was anarchy in a ruined country. 'He has restored vigour to that which was ruined among the eternal monuments. He has put down heresies and Truth has crossed the Two Lands. He has made it stable. Necessary things were in a wretched condition and the world was as at its beginning, when for its sake His Majesty as King of Upper Egypt appeared'. 'The possessions of the gods lay waste from Elephantine to the Delta. Their sanctuaries were in an unhappy state and their fields were going to rack and ruin, overgrown with weeds. Their abodes were utterly destroyed, their sacred enclosures became public footpaths. The world was defiled, the gods absent, the world was quite forgotten by them'. 'If messengers were sent to the Phoenician coast to enlarge Egypt's frontiers, they could avail no way at all. If recourse was had to the god to entrust things to his control, he did not come . . .'[12]

Aten's cult was not however entirely forbidden. The monuments formerly erected at Karnak by Akhenaten were respected and even added to.[13] The new reign sought to bring about social and religious peace, and to make amends for the excesses of the previous reign. The king nominated the priests and prophets of Amun from among the sons of Theban notables; but he kept Ay as vizier. The latter's presence proved that Aten and his followers were still powerful at Thebes.

Ay's rival, General Horemheb, a man of complex ambitions, watched all the Atenian reigns fade out before he himself seized power. A great soldier, he had just led a victorious expedition in Palestine, the only province that remained faithful to Egypt, and the last bulwark against the rising surge of the Asian advance. A skilful administrator, he reigned as ruler in Memphis, as his tomb bears witness, one of the grandest of the period, which depicts his deeds. Thanks to his triumphant campaign, he restored the tribute due to the king, who decorated him in a splendid ceremony. He seems, however, to have preserved his freedom of action by remaining at Memphis where he possessed great authority.

Egypt had lost nearly all her Asian provinces; but she still held Nubia, governed from Nekhen to Napata by Viceroy Huy. In his tomb we see him presenting the king with the tribute won by Horemheb in Nubia and at Retenu in Syria.[14] For the first time since the reign of Amenophis III the town of Thebes once more beheld such glittering festivities, and we can imagine the general rejoicings they inspired.

From the Nile bank where the Viceroy's glittering barge and those holding the tribute were anchored, a brilliant procession wended its way towards the palace. The crowd which was packed all along the route shouted at the sight of the black chiefs with their plume head-dresses, followed by their sons in Egyptian costumes. A Nubian princess passed in her chariot drawn by a pair of dwarf bullocks; over her head was a huge parasol made of ostrich-feathers; her dark brown skin showed through the white tunic.

Before her went Negro porters dressed in Egyptian style but with loincloths of vivid colours; on their heads they had stuck feathers into their amusing round wigs. They all bore fine vases full of gold, jasper, and malachite. An attendant led a giraffe, and this strange creature caused general hilarity. The bearded Syrians with their long embroidered robes were less appealing; but their gifts were as splended as those of the Nubians.

They brought handsome and smart stallions as well as a lion; they carried ornamented vases and dishes heaped with lapis lazuli. The magnificent cortége rejoiced the hearts of the Egyptians, who saw in the riches come to refill the treasuries of Amun and king the pledge of a return to former prosperity.

In the Palace the king was seated on his golden throne in ceremonial garments. Surrounded by his dignitaries, he received Huia, who with pen in hand, the insignia of his office, bowed respectfully while presenting the Nubians and Syrians who made obeisance at the throne's foot.

But in spite of the rejoicings and receptions the young ruler felt isolated in the old palace of Malkata, which had been reopened and hastily renovated for him. They who had known the charming ease of Akhenaten's court could not but feel tedium and undue length in the court etiquette, the great religious rites at Karnak or in the new temple south of the city, where restorations and enlargements had been resumed. Old uncle Ay was indeed there, someone they had always known; indeed he was the real master of the situation. But the others, the high priest of Amun and his clergy, were patricians who intrigued for official posts and gravitated around the throne. Were they friends of foes?

Did the young couple nostalgically recall the happy hours once spent in the maternal palace, when as children they played in the sycamore shade, in the 'green paradise of childhood loves'? Besides, their love-making had not been blessed. Twice the young wife had produced still-born babies, the pitiful little bodies were laid in the tomb of their father, who was soon to join them.

Was his death due to natural causes of was it the result of some obscure plot? An examination of the mummy would perhaps answer these questions; but nothing has yet been published on the subject.[15] Many fanatics must have wanted the removal of the king who stood for traditions and beliefs they considered odious. The events following his death are not well known, but we have a document which throws a tragic light upon them and enables us to get inside what happened. In her distress the young widow wrote the following letter to the Hittite king: 'My husband is dead and I have no son. But I am told you have begotten many sons. If you sent me one of them, he could marry me. I might choose one of my servants, but to make one of them my husband horrifies me'. Suspicious, Suppilulimas sent a messenger to get fuller information; but another request came to him through the Egyptian ambassador and he let one of his sons set out. However the youth was attacked on the way, perhaps by emissaries of Horemheb, and died before reaching the Egyptian frontier.[16]

The servant who 'horrified' the poor young queen as a husband was none other than the aged Ay. By marrying the legitimate heiress to the Egyptian throne, the old renegade would establish his own rights to the royal succession. Did the ill-assorted marriage ever take place?[17] In the Theban tomb which he 'exchanged' with Tutankhamen, we see, not the queen, but the trusty Ty, his old wife, whose name is in a cartouche. We do not

XVII Preceding page: *Head of Smenkhkare on a canopic jar*
XVIII *Head of a ushabti of the Pharaoh Akhenaten*
XIX Right: *Statuette of a King (Tutankhaten ?)*

*XX  Tutankhamun and Ankhesenamun; cover of an ivory casket*

not know what became of Ankhesenamun; the anguished appeal of the young queen remains forever without answer.

On his accession, which must have caused an unheard of scandal among Amun's followers, Ay was more than seventy-two years old. He must have felt very sure of his position to dare to take over not only the poor young widow, but also his predecessor's temple and tomb. He hastily buried Tutankhamen in his own vault, and there in the tomb, besides sumptuous ritual objects and superb jewels, he laid out the all dead king's mementos, even the furniture and toys of his happy childhood at Akhetaten. No doubt he thus hoped to appease the dead man's soul in the other worls after having despoiled him so outrageously in this one. By the irony of chance, Tutankhamen's tomb is the only one in the Valley of kings which has come down intact to our own days. Its sensational discovery made an obscure ruler the most well-known Pharaoh in all Egyptian history.[18]

Ay remained on the throne for nearly four years, but we know almost nothing of his reign. Of all the supernumeraries in the Amarna interlude, he is the one whose personality appears both the strongest and the subtlest. If he were really the brother of Queen Tiy, as we are tempted to believe, his role at the side of the Atenian Pharaohs is easily explained. We should not see him simply as an ambitious man who denied his god and his faith in order to seize power; rather we should see him as one who tried to save what was possible, by establishing a reign of tolerance favourable to the restoration of internal peace in a country torn by half a century of discord.

Horemheb, his successor, lacked his breadth of spirit. In the energy with which he destroyed all traces of the heresy, razing its monuments, usurping those of Tutankhamen, effacing for ever the names of Akhenaten and his heirs, he revealed a relentlessness in which sentiment or loyalty had no place. But this persecution, political rather religious, in reality masked the dubious legitimacy of the new Pharaoh. It was probably with the aid of Amun's clergy, whose candidate he was, that he succeeded in grasping the crown. After providing proof of his orthodoxy, he was elected as the result of an oracle given by Amun, to whom Horus, the patron god of his birthplace, had presented him.[19]

Thus ended the Amarna interlude. Akhetaten, the Horizon of the Disk, was abandoned. Its palaces and temples were levelled to the ground by royal command. The statues of the heretic and his family were savagely mutilated. The royal tomb was pillaged, and the mummy, torn from its sarcophagus, was burnt and dismembered. In all the private tombs the name and the face of 'the Comely Child of Aten' were ruthlessly hammered away. Then the private houses in their turn were abandoned. Some owners, however, barricaded the gates of their estates in the hope of some day returning; others left in such a hurry they forgot to open the doors of the cattle-sheds or to let loose their hunting-dogs, whose wretched bones were later found in the kennels.

Only the 'Beauty of Aten's Beauties', 'the Beautiful one who came', has never been found. Nor has Nefertiti's burial place been yet discovered; it seems that she was not laid in her husband's tomb. Some jewels bearing her name however exist (e.g. the gold ring in the Louvre Museum). A tale is told that towards the close of the last century a group of men, carrying a gold coffin, were seen one day coming down the eastern desert mountains, and not long afterwards valuable objects with Nefertiti's name on them appeared for sale . . . Sometime, perhaps, excavators will find the last dwelling of the woman who never accepted defeat and who died alone, abandoned by all, in her Castle of Aten.[20]

Such then was the tragic fate of the most dishonoured man in Egypt's history, the Criminal of Akhetaten, and of those whom he drew with him into his adventure.

# EPILOGUE

The new sovereign, the last of the XVIIIth dynasty, was both a soldier and an administrator. He already exemplified the 'new style' of the monarchs that were to succeed him, who bore the names of Sethi or Ramses. But the good days of conquest were ended; from now on there were to be only defensive struggles, with Egypt opposed to a formidable foe, the Hittites.

Horemheb reigned thirty years; he was kept busy in Egypt herself, straightening out the anarchic situation bequeathed by the Atenian Pharaohs. He therefore gave up any idea of regaining the Asian Empire and signed a treaty with the Hittites, inaugurating the policy of Egyptian-Hittite alliance which was carried on by his Ramessid successors. The period of peace allowed the Pharaoh to devote himself to internal affairs of Egypt. He began by publishing a decree aimed at suppressing corrupt practices and assuring a return to order. His conservative policy ensured that Amun's followers recovered all the offices of which they had been stripped by Akhenaten. The repressive measures were made as before in the name of Maat, Truth-Justice, and the latter showed herself particularly severe towards the guilty; the penalties were often out of all proportion to the offence. Pharaonic authority was henceforth replaced by a precise and impersonal system of regulations.

Horemheb had to pay dearly for his right to the throne; he gave up to the clergy and the tribunals the greater part of the supreme power formerly vested in the sovereign. His decree at the same time definitely established the dominance of the priesthood over the magistracy.[1]

The Amarna defeat thus ratified the victory of the clergy, who were to go on strengthening their position more and more at the expense of the throne. The last traces of Atenism were mercilessly suppressed by the triumphant reaction; the schismatic Pharaohs were excommunicated and their names were effaced from the royal annals. Amun was avenged.

Was the balance-sheet of the Amarna interlude then entirely negative? Certainly from the viewpoint of the Egyptian economy the experience was disastrous. The spoliation of Amun's property had enabled Akhenaten to build his Utopia. But the fabulous riches accumulated by several generations of Pharaohs had ended by being exhausted, and the treasury was no longer replenished from external resources. Even in an epoch so far from our own, when economic problems lacked the complexity that they own today, a great State could not allow itself the luxury of living as an autarchy.

A financial crisis could not but arise fairly quickly, and the famous tribute of the twelfth year was only a stopgap; it arrived too late to meet a deficit which daily grew worse. That is why the large-scale works, so gaily undertaken at the beginning of the revolution, were soon dropped for want of funds. The official constructions were never finished.

In a country where power is absolute, anarchy soon takes over when the central control weakens. No sooner was Akhenaten dead than the house of cards collapsed. The complete breakdown shows clearly that the revolution had never managed to drive any deep roots; the Atenian faith, born in a coterie of intellectuals, had never touched the people. The latter went automatically back to the ancestral beliefs which they had never really thrown off and which they could now freely practice again.

The cult of Aten was the personal cult of the royal family and it died with that family. To endure and prevail, a religious movement come out of the people; it must emerge as a hope offered to the oppressed; it must guarantee another world where injustices will be wiped out. That beyond, the kingdom of Osiris, had been abolished by Aten's intolerance without being replaced by some other belief. We have seen that in the tombs of Amarna, the dead man continued to enjoy benefactions from Aten on the threshold of his eternal abode; the kingdom of the dead was passed over in silence. As the years went on, many of the adepts of the new religion must have regretted the guarantees of eternal life supplied by the old system.

The doctrine of Aten has sometimes been criticised for its lack of ethical interests. Some Egyptologists assert that the king conceived a totally materialist creed and that the god's name must be taken in its literal meaning; in short, that Aten was more concrete and less spiritualized than any god of Egypt.[2] But in such a highly civilized country as Egypt of this period, morality was no longer necessarily a part of religion; it was merely placed under its protection. In banishing the other gods, Akhenaten had not thereby rejected the immemorial wisdom of Egypt; on the contrary he did his best to incorporate it in his religious teaching. In Ay's tomb we find some indications that tend to support this view. Aten is named 'Lord of Justice'; Ay describes himself as scrupulously loyal to the king who establishes Truth in him, and adds that 'he looks on lies as an abomination'. Later he adds, 'It is my works and my excellent character that have raised me to my present position', and, 'O my Lord, who establishes man, directs his life, and creates a happy fate for his favoured one so that his heart lives in Truth and lies are his abomination. How fortunate is he who hearkens to the doctrine of Life'.[3]

Another cause of the revolution's failure was not so much the fact of its creating a unique and visible god, as the fact its abolishing the other divinities. When he suppressed all the gods, Akhenaten in reality wanted to crush the most powerful one, whose clergy held power in their sole hands and barred his way forward. It was this political entanglement which from the outset undermined the spiritual ideal that the king sincerely wanted to foster.

91 Preceding page: *Seated portrait of General Horemheb as a scribe*

91 Preceding page: *Seated portrait of General Horemheb as a scribe*

92 Top left: *Detail of a procession (?)*
93 Bottom left: *The King bringing an offering*
94 Top: *A Mazoi-soldier of the Royal escort*
95 *Head of an Asiatic prisoner (?)*

96  Cover of a cosmetic box

The idea of a unique god was never foreign to Egyptian thought. As early as the Old Kingdom, God (with a capital G) had coexisted with a geographical polytheism inherited from the cults of prehistoric times. This God was that of a morality tinged with mysticism. He was a God both omniscient and good, living in the heart of any man able to hear his voice. In Chaldea also, the two conceptions (a single god and a polytheism) moved on side by side without one driving the other out. Here we touch on a movement of ideas which was general in all the Near East and which went on for centuries.

Some thinkers have attempted to see in Atenism the earliest manifestation of mon-otheism in history, even the source of Judaic monotheism and so of all modern religions. The main argument for this thesis lies in the remarkable parallel between Akhenaten's hymn and Psalm 104 of the Bible. It has been suggested that the correspondences neces-sarily indicate a direct connexion and that the Hebrew psalmists knew the Atenian hymn. Some scribe in the Asian city which was exalted into an image of Egypt's capital must have copied the hymn; and that hymn, translated into Semetic dialect, served as an inspiration for the psalmists five hundered years later.[4]

There may indeed be some extraordinary concordances between the two texts; but we for our part are inclined to see there, not a direct link, but the expression of a parallel influence originating in a yet earlier common source.[5] We must keep in mind that the Near East comprised at this period two centres of civilization, Egypt and Babylonia, whose influences flowed out in variable proportions (according to the period in question) over the neighbouring regions. Babylonian civilization knew an even wider diffusion than Egyptian; only Byblos in the Near East was wholly submitted to the latter.

Thanks to a common script and language, thanks also to the use of small clay tablets easy to carry, the literature and religious ideas of the Mesopotamian countries were prop-agated from early times all through the Near East. We have already noted that the meeting places for Egyptians and Mesopotamians were the ports of Syria and Palestine, where all races, all cultures, mingled and clashed. Egypt herself was also affected by new ideas when, from the time of Amenophis III, Chaldean scribes came in and settled there, to write and translate the Pharaohs' correspondence. They brought their libraries with them. As among the Hittites and the Mitannians, translations of the Epic of Gil-gamesh and other poems were recited in the fashionable coteries. Soon the students at Armana made them the subject of their own versions.[6] Over the centuries the epics and religious poems of the east were copied and recopied; their metaphors and their poetic view of the nature of things became the literary leit-motives of the whole ancient world. Egypt was no exception; the poetry of the New Kingdom lost the sobriety and austerity of earlier times. Secular poems, simultaneously direct and subtle, were imbued with the picturesque, with sentiment and charm. The same accents were heard in the hymns to Aten, in which the mythological allusions, the verbalism and the repetitions of the usual Pharaonic hymns, have all disappeared.[7]

The single god of Akhenaten is the god of the calendar, 'who creates and measures time'. 'As solar god, as god who created the heavens and all living beings', wrote R. Ber-thelot, 'he resembles Marduk who, five hundred years earlier, reigned in the Babylon of Hammurabi, when the solar calendar was substituted for the lunar one, The enumeration of months, years, and days, the way of characterizing the supreme god as master of time, remind us in a singular way of the ancient Chaldean formulas.'[8]

Monotheism is solidly established only where the concept of the unity of the universe has been formed and stabilized by a sidereal and mathematical calendar, which controls that of agricultural life. Such a concept had never come about in Egypt. Only in Mesopotamia and on the plateaus which dominated it, was the solar god transformed in a lasting way into a unique being who had created and who maintained the universal order—terrestrial and sidereal, physical and moral.

Berthelot adds, 'It was probably from Iran and also from certain forms of Babylonian thought that there comes above all the idea of the unity of God, or more precisely the idea of a unique god who at the same time is a personal god: that is, the monotheist idea'.[9]

It is then more than probable that in working out his religious reform Akhenaten was aware of the monotheist ideas which were developing in the New East. In choosing Aten, Rē's emanation, as sole god, he could rally to his side both the Egyptians and the Syrians who saw in Aten a deity close to their Adonai, Lord of Byblos. To bring these theological ideas to life there was needed the exalted enthusiasm of Akhenaten, his religious fervour, which alone could draw the masses over to a new ideal. But the passionately mystical sense of nature, which suddenly appeared in the metaphors and effusions of the hymns, and which was expressed in art by an entirely new aesthetic, could not be the work of a single man. Whence then came these accents, that exaltation, those exaggerations, those undulating lines, those ararbesques of bodies, which almost culminate in abstraction? These characteristics, completely *foreign* to Egyptian culture, belong to another current of civilization, which we shall try to make out.

In our first chapter we noted that the Mitannians belonged to the Indo-European race whose migrations in the second millenium spread east as well as west of the Iranian plateau (whence the name Aryan). In Mesopotamia they were preceded by the Hurrians and by the Kassites who finally settled in Babylonia. Even after establishing themselves in Asia Minor they retained their Aryan names and gods, as did their Iranian and Indian cousins, while adopting the language of the indigenous population among whom they installed themselves.[10] As excavations have not yet been organized in Mitanni (the region lying between Turkey, Irak, and Syria), we know Mitannian civilization only by its manifestations on the empire's periphery and in the neighbouring countries. We must therefore make our inquiry into its elements by indirect means, examining what we know of Indo-European peoples in general and what remained of them in Iran and India. The literary sources are the *Avesta* on the one hand and the *Rg-Veda* on the other: works which have very close affinities and witness to the nature-based character of Aryan religion.[11]

The most ancient Indian documents go back precisely to the first half of the second millenium, when Aryan tribes invaded India from the north-east, bringing with them the rudiments of the Veda's religion. 'We find in the Vedic songs memories of a life that might have been led very far from Hindustan, far in both time and space. Asianic elements seem mingled with Indian elements. There is a tendency to carry back certain parts to the Hittite period.'[12] Some scholars have supposed that the cults in question

170

swarmed out of India as far as the borders of Cappadicia; but it seems more plausible, writes Massom-Oursel, to find in them 'evidence of the movement of proto-Aryans into Asia Minor and into Syria'. The oldest religious texts of Persia and India, he adds, 'thus testify to a community of language and thought which guarantees a common origin'.

The evidence of the early link of the two Aryan systems is necessary, it seems to us, if one is to see more than a mere figment of the imagination in the comparison we are about to make. We have the right to assume that the Vedic songs (transcribed very much later into Sanscrit) were extremely closely-related to the Mitannian religious poems; and we hope that the day when these latter are discovered, written in the Hurrian or the Akkadian scripts, will confirm our hypothesis. Here are a few passages from The Vedic hymns compared with strophes from the Atenian hymns.

| *Aten* | *Rg-Veda* |
|---|---|
| Thou risest in beauty in the horizon of the sky. | Arise! Come onwards! you shine as the sole king. |
| Your rays, embrace the lands to the borders of your creation.<br>You are far, but your rays are on the earth. | With your light, purifying and protecting god, you cover the earth which bears men, you flood the sky, the vast air, and you gaze down on all that is. |
| When you rise, you dispel darkness. You have made the sky distant so that you may rise there and gaze down on all you have created. | |
| At dawn . . . you illuminate.<br>In the day you chase darkness away when you give your rays. | Dawn . . . It has come. The white and radiant one has come, and the black one has given up her seat. |
| You have created the earth according to your heart.<br>Then, wildbeasts, all that is in the sky, all that flies with wings. | You it is that have given to water-creatures their home in water. Wild beasts are spread along the steppes. Forests are for the birds. |
| You have set every man in his place and supplied his needs.<br>To each his food and his length of life. | All birds, all cattle go to their resting-places.<br>Savitr distributed beings according to their places. |
| To all you have created you give the breath of life. | The living breath is come to us. |
| You are the span of life by yourself. | We are at the turn where life is pro-longed. |

The agreement between these two texts seems to us more convincing than that between the Aten hymn and Psalm 104. These naturalistic poems could be interchanged; they both express the same love of nature, the same fervour towards the god who distributes earthly benefits. As with the hymns of Amarna, the Vedic hymns accompanied offerings of flowers and fruits, which were made in the open air, facing the sun. If the Mitannians worshipped Mitra, Indra, Varuna, it seems obvious that they must have preserved the ancestral hymns which glorified them. It is then likely enough that when Akhenaten composed his hymns (perhaps with Ay's collaboration), he *was acquainted with* the religious poems of Mitanni. They inspired in him the natureworship which was foreign to the Egyptian mentality, but which provided the very basis of his revolution. He added to that worship his own ideal of universal brotherhood by citing the distant regions of his empire and incorporating them in his prayer. His description of the countries where 'the Nile in the sky strikes the hillsides with its waters', shows how well he was informed about the Asian regions where he himself had never been. If Nefertiti was a Mitannian, as we are convinced, we have a further argument in favour of our comparison; and the leading role she played at the Pharaoh's side, attested by the representations and the texts at Amarna, allows us to suppose that she took a considerable part in the translation and explanation of the Mitannian poems which she had known from childhood.

Deeply affected by oriental natureworship, Akhenaten conceived a poetry of Franciscan tenderness in the description of flowers 'enraptured by the divine face', beasts 'leaping on their feet', and birds that 'fly for joy', beating their wings in praise of the living sun. The artists at Amarna had no difficulty in carrying this love of life into their paintings and sculptures. Never before had the delight of the vegetal and animal kingdoms been expressed with such warm sympathy.

But it was in sculpture in the round, the essentially Egyptian art form, once it was freed from the expressionist tendencies imposed by the Pharaoh at the outset of his reign, that the sculptors of Amarna conveyed with the utmost felicity the deepgoing sensuousness of oriental poetry. The female nudes swell with the fecundating sap of nature, which encloses them like a clinging liana in the continuous arabesque of the modelling; even the hardest stones express the palpitating and rich life of bodies, the warmth of skin, the pensive gentleness of faces.

This plastic beauty, fragile and tender, is both sensual and impregnated with spirituality; it belongs not only to a new art but also to a new aesthetic which leaves an enduring mark on Egyptian art of later periods.

Thus the balancesheet of the Amarna adventure provides also a positive side. It was not an unrelated phenomenon in the immemorial unfolding of Egyptian civilization. Despite itself, the latter carried on elements from what had happened. Even in the religious sphere Akhenaten's attempt at monotheism left its traces. Each local god regathered his sanctuaries and his worshippers, yet had henceforth no choice but to come closer to this nameless power, this *unknowable* god, of whom all earthly and traditional forms were only limited aspects. As we noted at the beginning of the book, the Egyptian gods were soon to be no more than different designations of a single divine entity.

The spirituality of the Atenian faith survived also in certain ways of thought, and

*XXI  Negros bringing tribute*

XXIII  *Head of a statue of the god Amun*
XXIV  Next page: *Statuette of a gazelle*

the humane and beneficient qualities of Aten were now attributed to Amun and other gods. A scribe of the Theban necropolis prayed to Amun as 'He who comes to the silent, who saves the disinherited, who gives life to all those he loves . . .' Another wrote, 'When I cry to you in my distress, you come and save me'. This new accent, this humility, is the sort of thing that belongs to periods of decadence when noble souls seek comfort and protection from a divinity embodying Truth and Justice. Similar aspirations were expressed in the tenth century B.C. in a treatise of highly-elevated thought, *The Teachings of Amenemope*, from which the *Book of Proverbs* borrowed many passages. Thus was propagated throughout the Near East the moral code fashioned over the centuries on the banks of the Nile.

The aesthetic of Amarna art, become a mannerism, persisted in Ramessid art. The elongated form of shaven heads, the undulating grace of gestures, the elegance of bodies with fine wrists and ankles, even the linear arabesque, the almost abstract multiplication of curves—all this was to gain an extraordinary impulse in the scenes of battle and hunt, that covered like an endless network, the walls of Theban temples. Sculpture in the round also showed the mark of Amarna. We no longer see the athletic Pharaohs with muscular torsos of the early New Kingdom. The most warlike of Egyptian monarchs, Ramses II, under his battle-helmet, shows the bent head and meditative countenance bequeathed by his predecessor. And so, despite the hatred and vindictiveness displayed by the Theban restoration in smashing up the monuments of heresy, the 'Conquered One of Amarna' could not be prevented from handing on to his successors many elements drawn from his revolution, of which, the most imponderable was doubtless a new consciousness.

The Ramessid Pharaohs restored to Egypt her imperial glory, but their victories could not prevent, they merely delayed, the empire's inevitable decay. The empire itself was personified in Ramses II. His long reign, his numerous progeny, his gigantic monuments and the epic tales about his death, turned him into a legendary figure, whose immense shadow, spread over the history of the Nile Valley. But in spite of the propaganda and the mania for things of colossal size, which he showed and which were in fact only signs of inner weakness, the throne did not inspire the old respect and tended towards an uneasy and exacting form of intolerance. Henceforth, the law was obliged to resort to magical practices. The post-Amarna period indeed saw a great increase in the use of magic: the effects of a troubled period in which men felt the need for some external help. Sorcery was invoked to ward off disastrous events. In losing self-confidence, Egypt lost security. Life in the Otherworld took on a renewed importance and Osiris reigned as Lord in the burial-places, which were dug deep in the western mountains. A vast funerary and magical literature covered the walls of endless corridors to help the dead man by every kind of material means in reaching the Fields of Ialu where his posthumous life was to be spent.

It was the reign of the grandiose, but also of the mysterious; the reign of refinement and superstition, of luxury and cruelty. Egypt had become an Oriental nation. Her destiny was henceforth inextricably bound up with that of the civilizations of the Near East. She still produced masterpieces; she was still sumptuous and radiant; but her art had irretrievably lost the restraint and grace which had given a unique lustre to the beginnings of the XVIIIth dynasty.

Throughout the vicissitudes of her long history Egypt continued to feel regret for that golden age. In the XXVIth dynasty she even attempted a 'Renaissance' by leaning for a last time on her great past. That was the final reaction, against infiltrations foreign to her genius, of a civilization that was nearing its deathbed.

EGYPT

| B.C. | Amenhotep III (1408–1371) | Regnal Year | Amenhotep IV–Akhenaten (1371–1356) | Smenhkhere (1358–1355) |
|---|---|---|---|---|
| 1408 | Accession to the throne | 1 | | |
| 1407 | Marriage. Hunts | 2 | | |
| | Birth of Satamen (?) | 3. | | |
| | Nubian Expedition. | 5. | | |
| 1399 | Marriage with Gilukhepa | 10. | | |
| 1398 | Pleasure Lake | 11. | | |
| 1397 | Inauguration of Aten Temple | 12. | | |
| 1394 | Birth of Amenhotep IV (?) | 15. | Birth (1394 ?) | |
| 1384 | Birth of Bakitaten (?) | 25. | | |
| 1383 | Babylonian Marriage | 26. | | |
| 1381 | Marriage with Satamen (?) | 28. | | |
| 1380 | Birth of Smenkhkere (?) | 29. | | |
| 1379 | First Heb-Sed | 30. | | |
| 1375 | Second Heb-Sed | 34. | | |
| 1374 | Visit of Goddess Ishtar | 35. | | |
| 1373 | Arrival of Tadukhepa (?) | 36. | Marriage (?) | |
| 1372 | Third Heb-Sed | 37. | 1. Co-Regency and Birth of First Daughter | |
| 3371 | Death of the King | 38. | 2. Tushratta's Letter of Condolence | |
| 1370 | | | 3. Inauguration of Temple of Aten, Karnak. Birth of Second Daughter | |
| 1369 | | | 4. Foundation of Akhetaten. Birth of Third Daughter | |
| 1368 | | | 5. Heb-Sed of Aten and Akhetaten | |
| 1367 | | | 6. Removal to Akhetaten. Birth of Fourth Daughter | |
| 1366 | | | 7. Babylonian Marriage (?) | |
| 1365 | | | 8. Birth of Tutankhaten (?) | Birth (1365 ?) |
| 1364 | | | 9. Change of Aten's Name. Birth of Fifth Daughter (?) | |
| 1362 | | | 11. Birth of Sixth Daughter (?) | |
| 1361 | | | 12. Foreign Tribute. Visit of Queen Tiy | |
| 1360 | | | 13. Marriage of Meretaten (?) | Marriage with Meretaten (?) |
| 1359 | | | 14. Death of Meretaten (?) | |
| 1358 | | | 15. Quarrel with Nefertiti (?) | Co-Regency (?) |
| 1357 | | | 16. Marriage with Ankhesepaaten | Voyage to Memphis and Thebes |
| 1356 | | | 17. Birth of little Ankhesepaaten | |
| 1355 | | | 18. Death of the King | Death of Co-Regent. |
| 1353 | | | | 1. |
| 1351 | | | | 3. |
| 1346 | | | | 5. |
| 1344 | | | | 9. |

| Tutankhamen (1355–1346) | Ay (1346–44) | Horemheb (1344 (?)–1314) | |
|---|---|---|---|
| | | | About 1400: Accession of Tushratta of Mitanni; his intrigues in Syria |
| | | | About 1390: Accession of Kadashman-Enlil I, King of Babylon |
| | | | About 1385: Accession of Suppululiumas, King of the Hittites; pacification of Anatolia |
| | | | About 1372: Death of Kadashman-Enlil I; accession of Burraburiash as King of Babylon |
| | | | About 1370: Accession of Assuruballit I, King of Assyria |
| Birth (1365 ?) | | | About 1366: Assassination of Tushratta |
| | | | About 1365: Assuruballit annexes a part of Mitanni |
| | | | Breakdown of Egyptian Dominion in Palestine |
| | | | First Treaty between Egypt and the Hittites |
| Accession to the throne Marriage with Ankhenpaaten Death of Nefertiti. Departure for Thebes Death in Thebes. His wife writes to the Hittite King. Her marriage with Ay (?) | Accession of Ay Death of Ay | Accession of General Horemheb | About 1355: Suppililiumas takes Carchemish; anarchy in Palestine; Mitanni vassal of the Hittite King<br>About 1350: Death of Burraburiash II, King of Babylon<br>About 1345: Death of Suppiluliumas; he is succeeded by Mursil II. |

# GENEALOGY OF THE XVIIIth DYNASTY

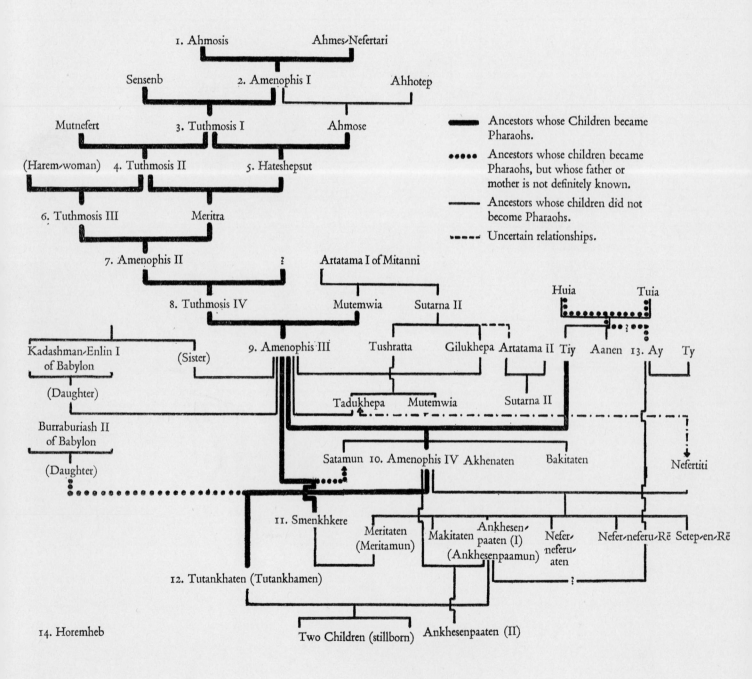

Ancestors whose Children became Pharaohs.

Ancestors whose children became Pharaohs, but whose father or mother is not definitely known.

Ancestors whose children did not become Pharaohs.

Uncertain relationships.

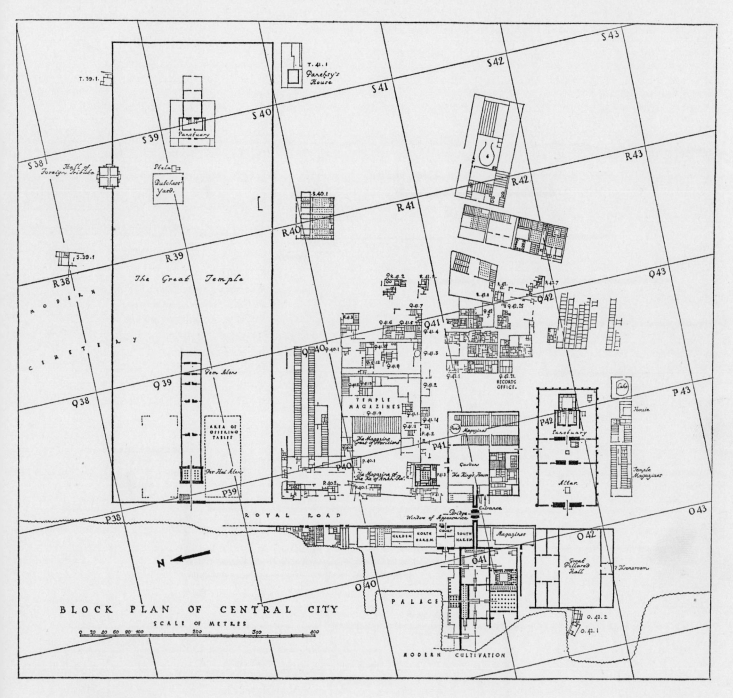

BLOCK PLAN OF CENTRAL CITY

SCALE OF METRES

AKHETATEN

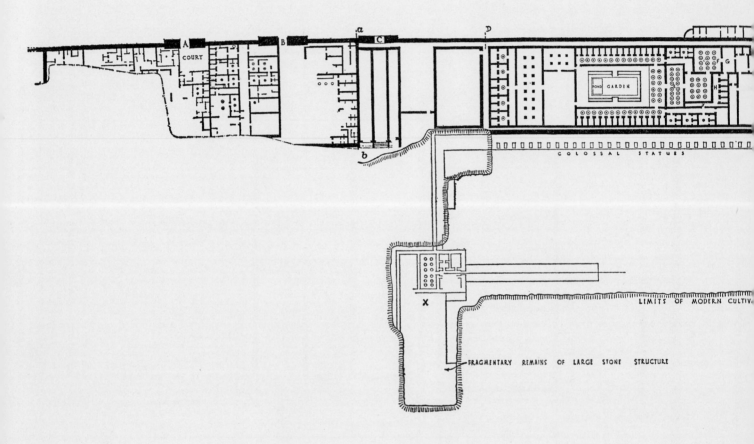

COLOSSAL STATUES

POND GARDEN

LIMITS OF MODERN CULTIV.

FRAGMENTARY REMAINS OF LARGE STONE STRUCTURE

SCALE OF METRES

0  5  10  15  20  25  30  35  40  45  50      60      70      80      90      100      110      120

GREAT PALACE

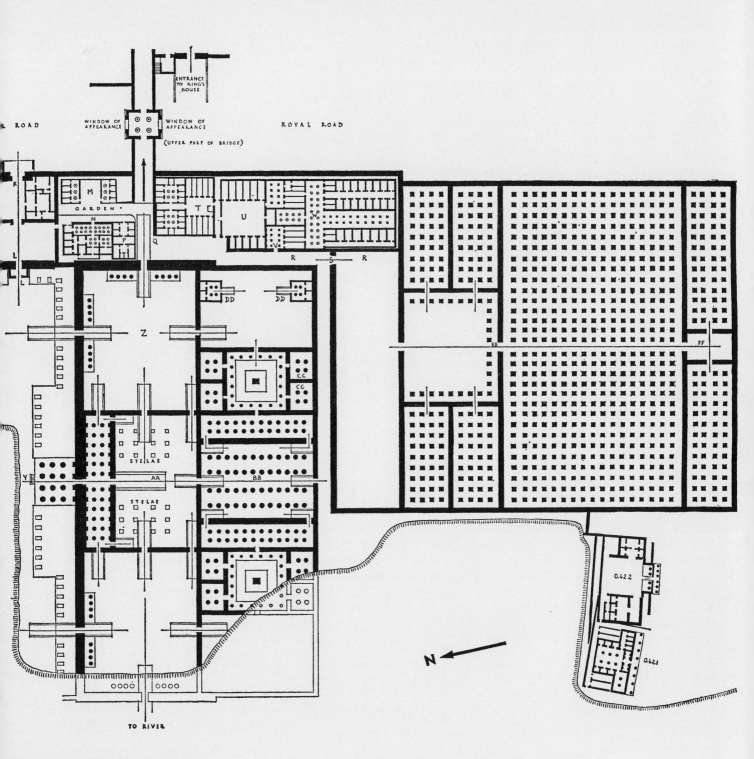

ENTRANCE
TO KING'S
HOUSE

WINDOW OF
APPEARANCE

WINDOW OF
APPEARANCE

ROYAL ROAD

(UPPER PART OF BRIDGE)

K

M

GARDEN

N

P

Q

T

U

V

L

L

DD

DD

R

S

R

Z

CC

CC

EE

FF

Y

STELAE

AA

BB

STELAE

0.422

0.421

N

TO RIVER

# RESTORED PLAN

# ABBREVIATIONS USED IN THE NOTES

A.E. = *Ancient Egypt*, London, 1914–34.

A.R. = *Ancient Records of Egypt*. Historical Documents from the earliest Times to the Persian Conquest collected, edited and translated with Commentary by J. H. Breasted.

A.S.A. = *Annales du Service des Antiquités de l'Egypte*, Le Caire.

B.I.F.A.O. = *Bulletin de l'Institut français d'Archéologie Orientale*, Le Caire.

Cat. Gén. = *Catalogue Général des Antiquités égyptiennes du Musée du Caire*, Le Caire.

Chronique = *Chronique d'Egypte*, Bruxelles.

E.E.F. = *Egypt Exploration Fund*, London.

E.E.S. = *Egyptian Exploration Society*, London.

J.E.A. = *Journal of Egyptian Archaeology*, London.

J.N.E.S. = *Journal of Near Eastern Studies*, Chicago.

M.D.O.G. = *Mitteilungen der Deutschen Orient-Gesellschaft*, Berlin.

M.I.A.F.O. = *Mémoires de l'Institut Français d'Archéologie Orientale du Caire.*

Porter & Moss = B. Porter & R. Moss, *Topographical Bibliography of Ancient Egyptian hieroglyphic Texts, Reliefs and Paintings*, Vol. I–VII, Oxford, 1927–51.

# NOTES

## INTRODUCTION

[1] See R. Engelbach, 'Material for a Revision of the History of the Heresy Period of the XVIIIth Dynasty', *A.S.A.*, 1940, XL, pp. 133–65.

[2] Cited by Emile Léonard in the Preface of *Histoire Universelle* (Encyclopédie de la Pléiade, Paris), I, p. XVII.

[3] See J. Yoyotte, *Dictionnaire de la Civilisation égyptienne* (Paris, Fernand Hazan), 1959, p. 25.

[4] See A. Scharff, 'Egyptian Portrait-Sculpture', *Antiquity*, 1937, p. 174.

[5] Cited by F. Daumas, 'Amour de la Vie et sens du Divin dans l'Égypte ancienne', *Etudes Carmélitaines*, 1952, p. 92–141.

[6] Emile Léonard, *op. cit.*, p. XVIII.

## CHAPTER I

[1] *Iliad*, IX, 383–4.

[2] A. Parrot, *Sumer*, p. 3 (L'Univers des Formes, Paris), 1960.

[3] *A.R.* II, 467. In the narration of the 6th campaign of Tuthmosis III in Asia, it says 'The sons of Princes and their brothers were then taken to Egypt as hostages. When one of them died . . . His Majesty had the habit of placing his son in his place'.

[4] E. Drioton et J. Vandier, *Les Peuples de l'Orient méditerranéen*. II, L'Egypte (Les Presses Universitaires de France, 4th ed. Paris), 1962, p. 410. According to a letter from E. Edel to the authors, the identification proposed by Jensen (*Z.Ä.S.* 1890, p. 114) from a tablet found in Amarna, has been erroneously read. The decisive proof is still missing.

[5] For a long time it was believed that Yuia was Prince of Djahi in Syria, after an inscription on a vase in the Fitzwilliam Museum of Cambridge (see H. R. Hall in *P.S.B.* 1913, 35, p. 63); but according to E. Meyer, *Geschichte des Altertums*, II, p. 323, followed by C. Aldred, *J.E.A.*, 1957, p. 31, note 3, the inscription is apocryphal. The ethnical type of Yuia is however strongly foreign, as his mummy proves (see J. E. Quibell, *Tomb of Yuaa and Thuia*, in *Cat. gén.* 1908, p. 68); see also Elliot Smith, *The Royal Mummies, idem*, 1912, no. 61076) concerning the parentage of Smenkhkere's mummy: both (i.e. Yuia and Smenkhkere) have an 'armenoid' jaw.

[6] The name of Yuia lacks an Egyptian consonance; the numerous transcriptions which it has been given suggest that it sounded foreign to Egyptian ears, who reproduced it phonetically (see J. E. Quibell, *op. cit.*). The name permits us to tell if a person is of Asiatic origin; and the criterion can be unreservedly accepted for the beginning of the New Kingdom, J. Janssen tells us, in 'Fonctionnaires sémites au service de l'Egypte', *Chronique*, 1951, p. 50.

[7] See C. Aldred, in *J.E.A.*, XLIII, p. 31. The titles and functions of Yuia were probably hereditary. Aldred compares them to those of a certain Yey of whom there exists an shawabti in the Metropolitan Museum of New York, who perhaps could have been an ancestor?

[8] A recent theory, based on an opinion expressed at one time by Maspero (*Guide du Visiteur au Musée du Caire*, 1915, p. 369), sees in Tiy's parents Africans of the race of the Maazehs. If such were the case, their descendents of whom we possess mummies (Smenkhere and Tutankhamen) should present negroid features: which has not been scientifically proved. This theory, which lacks a serious foundation, appears mainly to seek to flatter a certain nationalism hoping to establish the African character of Pharaonic civilization.

[9] See Droiton & Vandier, *op. cit.*, p. 453ff.

[10] A. Bataille, 'Aménothès, fils de Hapou à Deir el Bahari', *B.S.F.E.*, no. 3, 1950, p. 11.

[11] J. Pirenne, 'Le Statut de l'étranger dans l'ancienne Égypte', *Recueil de la Societé* Jean Bodin, IX (Ed. de la Librairie Encyclopédique Bruxelles) 1938, pp. 93–103.

[12] J. Pirenne, 'Le droit international sous la XVIII° dynastie', *Rev. internationale des droits de l'Antiquité* (Bruxelles, 3° série, T.V.) 1958.

[13] W. Preiser, 'Zum Völkerrecht der vorklassichen Antike', *Archiv des Völkerrechts* (Tübingen, 4. Band, 3 Heft) 1954.

[14] For the description of the Malkata Palace, see W. Stevenson-Smith, *The Art and Architecture of Ancient Egypt* (Penguin Books, Baltimore) 1958, who summarizes the preliminary reports of excavations by the Metropolitan Museum (see also p. 274, note 2). For the complete bibliography, see Porter & Moss. II, p. 160.

[15] Th. M. Davis, *The Tomb of Iouiya and Touiyou* (London, Constable & Co.) 1907.

[16] L. Borchardt, 'Ein Onkel Amenophis IV als Hoherpriest von Heliopolis.' *Z.A.S.* XLIV, p. 97.

[17] C. Aldred, 'The end of the Amarna period', *J.E.A.*, XLIII, p. 30–41. The author bases himself on the similarity of titles. Ay is also Master of Horse and Divine Father, but instead of being a chariot officer, Ay is a Captain of Infantry. There is also the comparison of names. Yui = Ay (see above note 7). But where we do not agree with the author, is when he sees in the Divine Father Ay, the father-in-law of Amenhophis IV, that is to say, the father of Nefertiti.

[18] N. de G. Davies, *The Tomb of the Vizier Ramose* (E.E.S., London) 1941. See also Porter & Moss, I, p. 105ff., for the bibliography.

[19] A. Moret, *Le Nil et la civilisation égyptienne* (Paris) 1926, p. 411.

[20] M. Eliade, *Mythes, Rêves et Mystères* (Paris, 1957, 2° ed) p. 13.

[21] R. Berthelot, *La Pensée de l'Asie et l'Astrobiologie* (Paris, Payot).

[22] Drioton & Vandier, *op. cit.*, Chap. III, *La Religion*.

[23] R. Berthelot, *op. cit.*

[24] A. Moret, *op. cit.* p. 369.

## CHAPTER II

[1] According to Maspero, *Histoire ancienne des peuples de l'Orient classique* (Paris) 1895–7, II, p. 316, Amenhophis III had had several sons, the eldest Tuthmosis having died prematurely. He had been High Priest of Ptah in Memphis and there exists a whip bearing his name in the Tutankhamen's treasure. In 1913, A. Gardiner discovered in Thebes a grave (no. 26) where we see *four* princes on the proprietor's knees. The name of only one was found, Ankh-kheper-uu-rē, the enthronement name of Smenkhkere (see *Bulletin of the Metropolitan Museum*, New York, Dec. 1923, pp. 42–43). If Amenophis IV celebrated his *heb-sed* at the same time as that of his god, i.e. in the year 6 of his reign, when he himself had reached 30 years of age, his birth went back to the twelfth year of his father's reign.

[2] *A.R.* II, 861 to 868.

[3] For each of these important events of his reign, Amenophis III (like his father Tuthmosis IV) had scarabs engraved: to commemorate his marriage to Queen Tiy, his hunting exploits in the Delta and to celebrate his weddings to foreign princesses as well as the construction of a pleasure lake. R. Engelbach, 'A Kirgipa Commemorative Scarab of Amenophis III', in *A.S.A.* 1940, XL, p. 659. This scarab is dated of the year 10 and gives the name of Queen Tiy's parents. It describes the arrival of Princess Kirgipa, daughter of Shutarna, King of Mitanni and her suite. See also *A.R.* II, 866.

[4] S. A. B. Mercer, *The Tell-el-Amarna Tablets* (Toronto, MacMillan & Co of Canada Ltd) 1939. See also J. A. Knudtzon, *Die El-Amarna Tafeln* (Leipzig) 1907. These letters written in cuneiform characters on clay tablets, contain the official correspondence of Amenhetep III and his son with the Kings of Babylon, Assyria, Mitanni and Hatti and also the princes of the Aegean Islands and the Egyptian provinces of Asia. Their importance is capital, for they reveal the diplomatic life of the Mediterranean world of that period.

[5] Elliot Smith, *op. cit.* no. 61074.

[6] *Idem.* The king's mummy is very well preserved thanks to a curious technique in which resin was injected

under the skin in order to pad the body and give it the corpulence it owned when alive. Intact, the head had been very carefully examined by the author.

[7] Several portraits of the Queen have been identified by means of inscriptions; a small ebony statuette in the Museum of Hildesheim (no. 53b), the pendant of that of her husband, a caricatural work representing the Queen grown stout with age; the colossal group in the Cairo Museum in which the features are conventional; a head coming from Sinai (Cairo, no. 38.257) where the oval shaped face shows almond shaped eyes, a thick and sulky mouth, cheeks still round and giving a youthful impression; the most beautiful example was found in the Palace of Gurob (Berlin, 21.834).

[8] A. W. Shorter, 'Historical Scarabs of Thutmosis IV and Amenophis III', *J.E.A.* XXVII, 1931, pp. 22–25. The text says that the Pharaoh Tuthmosis IV fought 'with the Aton before Him' . . . He went into Naharin and Karoy to bring the inhabitants of foreign countries as future subjects of the Aton for eternity'. The text is of the utmost importance for it gives us proof that Aten was not only already considered as a distinct form of the solar god by Tuthmosis IV, but was also adored as the God of Battles, ensuring victory to the Pharaoh and his domination over other peoples. Amenophis IV sought to fulfill the ambitions of his grand-father which, through the latter's premature death and with his own father's indolence, had been left unfulfilled.

[9] J. H. Wilson, *The Burden of Egypt* (Chicago) 1952. The author tells us that under Amenophis III a certain Ramose was Priest of Amen and at the same time steward of Aten's Temple. Another inscription begs the Pharaoh to ask Amen-Ra to give an offering to the 'Scribe of the Treasury of Aton's Temple'', whose name was Penbuy (see Glanville, *J.E.A.*, XV, 1929, p. 5).

[10] See above, note 2.

[11] A. Varille, *A.S.A.* XLL, 1941, pp. 651–7. Amenophis III would have justified his marriage with Satamun as the means of preserving for his descendants the purity of Tiy's blood, Tiy herself being now incapable of further conceptions. Amenhetep, Son of Hapu was named majordomo of Satamun and died in the year 31 of his Master's reign, at the time when Satamun was called 'royal daughter, royal spouse'. There exist several documents which confirm that Satamun was indeed the daughter of Tiy: on a box is written: 'born of the Great Royal Wife Tiy' (see also Newberry, *P.S.B.A.*, 1902, p. 246). According to Gauthier, *Livre des Rois* (Le Caire, II, p. 339) the name of Satamun is surrounded by a cartouche on a wooden seat in the tomb of Juia her grandfather, and also on the statue of Amenhetep, Son of Hapu.

According to Michailidis, *A.S.A.* XLV, 1947, pp. 123–5, a pendant bearing the names of Amenophis III and Satamun was found at Shiubt; it bears the King's cartouche followed by that of Satamun, 'to whom life has been given'. The name of the latter in a cartouche associated with the royal cartouche, to the exclusion of all others, corroborates the thesis of the union of Amenophis and his daughter.

[12] Among the arguments in favour of this hypothesis, we have the physical particularities of the mummy found in Tiy's tomb, which can only be that of Smenkhkere. The face shows certain differences with that of Amenhophis III, says E. Smith (*op. cit.* no. 61075, p. 55), but these differences are racial; Smenkhkere's face is armenoid and identical with that of Yuia (his great grandfather) while that of Amenophis III is Egyptian; however, we discover in both, the hereditary defect of the paternal line, the projecting incisors. On the other hand, Amenophis III also married, in the year 26, a Babylonian princess, sister of King Burraburiash II and aunt of that other princess who was later to marry Akhenaten. The former of these two princesses could have been the mother of Smenkhkere, while the other could have been the mother of Tutankhamen, as we suggested already in 1943 (see J. Capart etc., *Toutankhamon et son temps*, Bruxelles, 1943, p. 65). This double relationship would explain the great resemblance which is evident in the mummies of these two Pharaohs.

[13] Vide Chapter IV, p. 96, where we examine the mask (taken from life) of Nefertiti and her polychrome bust. In the latter, the Queen has a fresh and rosy skin, a straight nose and no resemblance whatever with the other members of the royal family. If Nefertiti was not Tadukhepa, she was still Queen and Tushratta would have mentioned her in his letters at the same time as he cited Tiy.

[14] The supporters of year 12 base themselves on the emendation of Erman (*Z.A.S.* 1889, p. 63) suggesting the reading 12 instead of 2; but they neglect the fact that Erman *retracted* the correction while Knudtzon was preparing his edition of the tablets. He then decided to definitely accept the year 2. As Gardiner, who is also convinced that one should read 2 and not 12 (*J.E.A.* XLIII, 1957, p. 13), points out, Tushratta's letters cover a period of short duration since they always mention the same ambassadors, both Mitannians and Egyptians. Furthermore Amenophis IV received the letter while he was residing in Thebes (Hayes, *J.N.E.S.X*, 1951, p. 180). From the year 6, he had taken the oath to never leave Akhetaten. Without proof to the contrary, we must accept as fact that in the year 12 he remained faithful to this oath and that he never returned to Thebes.

A recent work of E. F. Campbell Jr. *The Chronology of the Amarna Letters* (Baltimore, The John Hopkins Press, 1964) summarizes the whole problem, the author finally agreeing that it is indeed the year 2 that this letter dates from. Therefore, if we accept the year 2, all this built-up theory of a long co-regency between the two sovereigns falls to the ground as well as the hypothesis that Amenophis III was the father of Tutankhamen. The presence of monuments and portraits of the old King in Amarna in no way proves that he was personally there during his lifetime. Houses dedicated to dead Pharaohs, i.e. Tuthmosis I, Amenophis II and Tuthmosis IV were also found in Amarna; the presence of these names was simply due to the filial piety of Akhenaten (Gardiner *dixit*). If there had really existed a long co-regency, the name and the monuments of Amenophis III would certainly have been destroyed as were those of his son.

15 *A.R.* II, 934. See also A. Moret, *op. cit.* p. 371.

16 Ptahmosis was 'high prophet of Amun overseer of all the prophets of the South and the North, overseer of the city of Thebes, vizier of the entire Egypt'; see G. Legrain, *Recueil*, XXIX, p. 83 (cited by A. Moret, *Rois et Dieux d'Egypte*, Paris, 1923, p. 50). See also A. Varille, *B.I.F.A.O.*, 1931, XXX, p. 497-507.

17 Vide Marianne Doresse, 'Les Temples atoniens de la région thébaine', 'Orientalia, 1955, 24, pp. 113-35.

18 J. H. Breasted. *The Dawn of Conscience* (Scribner, New York) 1934, p. 278.

19 N. de G. Davies, *J.E.A.*, 1923, p. 151.

20 *idem*, *J.E.A.* 1923, pp. 132ff. Also A. Mekhitarian, *La Peinture égyptienne* (Paris, Skira) 1954.

21 N. de G. Davies, *The Tomb of the Vizier Ramose* (London) 1941. For the coloured reproductions of the paintings see Nina M. Davies, *Ancient Egyptian Paintings* (London) pl. XXI-XXIII.

22 This would imply that the new conception of reality had come about at Thebes, as was suggested by W. Stevenson-Smith, *op. cit.*, p. 181.

23 J. D. S. Pendlebury, *Yell-el Amarna* (London, Lovat, Dickson & Thomson Ltd) 1935.

24 According to Moret (*Le Nile, op. cit.* p. 373, note 3) this inscription is to be found in the tomb of the vizier Ramose but Davies (*op. cit.*) makes no mention of it whatever.

25 B. Gunn, 'Note on the Aten and his names', J. E. A., IX, 1923, p. 168ff.

26 F. LL. Griffith, *J.E.A.*, 1918, p. 61ff.

27 Dante, *Purgatorio*, Canto IX.

## CHAPTER III

1 W. M. Flinders Petrie, *Tell-el-Amarna* (London, Methuen & Co) p. 2. Also J. D. S. Pendlebury, *op. cit.*, p. XVII.

2 U. Bouriant, 'Deux jours de fouilles à Tell el-Amarna', *Mission archéologique francaise au Caire*, I, 1884, p. 1-22 *et Monuments pour servir à l'étude du culte d'Atonou*, M.I.F.A.O., VIII, I, by Bouriant, Legrain et Jéquier, 1903.

3 Petrie, *op. cit.*

4 N. de G. Davies, *The rock Tombs of El Amarna*, Archaeological Survey of Egypt, XIII to XVIII, London, 1903, to 1908.

5 L. Borchardt, 'Voruntersuchung von Tell el-Amarna', *M.D.O.G.*, 1907, no. 46, 50, 52, 55, 57. Also P. Timme, 'Tell el-Amarna, Voruntersuchung der Deutschen Ausgrabung', *idem* no. 31, 1917. H. Schäfer, 'Die Neuaustellung der Funde aus Amarna in Berliner Museen', *idem*, no. 63. By the same, 'Das Wesen der Amarna Kunst', *idem*, no. 64.

6 *The City of Akhenaten*, 3 volumes: I by T. E. Peet & L. Woolley, 1922; II by H. Frankfort & J. D. S. Pendlebury, 1933; III by J. D. S. Pendlebury and others, 1951 (Egypt Exploration Society, Oxford University Press, London).

7 *A.R.* II, 949 to 972: The Tell el-Amarna Landmarks.

8 There were two other Aten cities, one in Nubia on the West bank of the third Nile water-fall, Gem-Aten, and another in Syria. (See J. H. Breasted, History of Egypt, trans. Prof. Dr. Hermann Ranke, p. 217, Phaidon Press, 1954, Zürich.)

9 Pendlebury, *op. cit.* p. 98.

10 *The City of Akhenaten*, III, p. 22ff.

11 *The City of Akhenaten*, III, p. 60.

12 H. Ricke, *Der Grundriss des Amarna Wohnhauses* (Leipzig) 1932. For a concise description see Pendlebury, *op. cit.*, p. 101ff.

13 This house has been reconstituted from a model by Seton Lloyd, *J.E.A.*, 1933, XIX. Pendlebury describes it. *op. cit.* p. 102. pl. IV.

14 See Monu. pour servir au culte d'Atonou, I, p. 3ff.

15 Aldred (see Chap. I note 17) would like to prove that Ay was not only the uncle but the father-in-law of Akhenaten. He backs this theory by translating the title of Ty (Ay's wife) as step-mother to Nefertiti; the

latter would then have been Ay's daughter by a former marriage with a royal princess, while Mutnedjem would be his daughter by Ty, and so half-sister of Nefertiti. On the other hand, K. C. Seel, in 'King Ay and the close of Amarna Age', *J.N.E.S.*, 14, 1955, p. 168, keeps to the translation of Ty's title as 'nurse' which no longer allows him to believe that Nefertiti is Tadukhepa, daughter of the King of Mitanni. This does not seem to us to be a valid objection: a letter from Burraburiash to Akhenaten (no. 11) tells us that the princess asked for in marriage by the Pharaoh has an Egyptian governess, established at the Babylonian Court. Why should not Ty, nurse or governess of Tadukhepa (Nefertiti), have come from Mitanni into Egypt at the same time as the princess?

[16] Davies, *The rock Tombs . . .* IV, pl. XXII.

[17] *Idem.*

[18] *Idem,* IV, pl. XXIV, XXVI.

[19] *Idem,* tomb of Ay, VI, p. 16 to 25.

[20] Marcelle Werbrouck, *Les Pleureuses dans l'Egypte ancienne* (Bruxelles, Fondation Égyptologique Reine Elisabeth).

[21] Davies, *op. cit.* Tomb of Tutu, VI, pp. 7 to 15.

[22] A. Erman, *Die Religion der Ägypter* (Berlin), 1934.

[23] Davies, *op. cit.* tomb of Ahmes, III, p. 32.

[24] Pierre Gilbert, *La poésie égyptienne* (Bruxelles) 1943.

[25] Hymn to the Aten; tomb of Ay, Davies, *op. cit.* VI, XXVII.

[26] A. Moret, *Rois et Dieux d'Egypte* (Paris, 1923), p. 70.

## CHAPTER IV

[1] Preface to *Sumer* by A. Parrot (Paris) 1960.

[2] *The Mural Paintings of el Amarnah*, edited by H. Frankfort (E.E.S. London) 1929.

[3] See the preliminary report of L. Borchardt, *op. cit.*; no. 52. Also, by the same; *Das Atelier des Bildhauers Thutmes in Tell-el-Amarna* (Berlin, Herman).

[4] This description is not fanciful, being based on precise details found during the discovery.

[5] G. Roeder, *Lebensgrosse Tonmodelle aus einer altägyptischen Bildhauerwerkstatt, Jahrbuch des preussischen Kunstsammlungen* (Berlin) 1942, 62, p. 145ff. See also H. Schäfer, 'Amarna in Religion und Kunst', *Sendschrift des Deutschen Orient Gesellschaft*, 1923; H. O. Lange, *König Echnaton und die Amarna Zeit* (Munich) 1951.

[6] L. Borchardt, *op. cit.* p. 34. G. Roeder, *Waren die Künstler des Pharaonenreichs auch Persönlichkeiten?* (Berlin) 1947, pp. 198–204. The author still rejects the theory that the Amarna masks have been taken from life and without expressly saying so, inclines to Bissing's explanation. The latter suggests that these masks were studio studies which were not copied but were used for the execution of certain details. See also E. Buschor, *Bildnisstufen* (Munich 1947, Münchener Verlag).

[7] Comment les Egyptiens faisaient leurs statues?, *Chronique*, 26, 1938, and my long review of Roeder's book (see note 5), *Chronique*, 35, 1943, p. 107.

[8] H. Brummer, *Altorientalische Gesichtsmasken aus Gips in ihrem Zusammenhang mit der Kunst* (Berlin) 1954. At Gizeh were found skulls covered with a coat of plaster to preserve the features of the dead. This is the origin of the plaster cast. From the same period (IVth–VIth dynasty) date the funerary portrait-heads. Although their purpose was religious, these objects are works of art. They are to be compared with the bust of Ankh-haf (Boston Museum) where a fine layer of plaster has been modelled on the stone nucleus.

[9] See above Chapter I, note 17.

[10] Excavations of the E.E.S. 1932–3, published in *J.E.A.*, XIX, 1933 and in *City of Akhenaten.*

[11] Petrie, *op. cit.* p. 40.

[12] H. Schäfer, *Amarna*, pl. 8 and 9 and also Borchardt, *M.D.O.G.* 57, p. 14. This comparison may be confirmed by comparing with the small ebony statuette of the Brooklyn Museum.

[13] *The City of Akhenaten*, III, p. 203. This edifice has been described in Huya's tomb (Davies, *op. cit.* III); it had a courtyard with columns and between these thirty-two statues of Amenophis III, of Akhenaten, Tiy and Nefertiti.

[14] L. Borchardt, 'Porträts des Königin Mofre-ete', *Wiss. der D.O.G.*, 1923, 44, p. 32.

[15] There exists at the Boston Museum a series of statuettes of King Mycerinus of the IVth dynasty which show us the successive stages of the stone-carver's work. G. Reisner, *Mycerinus* (Cambridge, Mass) 1931.

[16] 'They (the Egyptians) do not conceive their statues from imagination as did the Greeks for, after having arranged and cut their stone, they carry out their work in such manner that all parts adapt themselves to each other down to the slightest detail. This is the reason for which they divide the human body in twenty-one parts

and a quarter and base on this the symmetry of the work. Thus, after the workmen have agreed on the height of the statue, they each work at home on the parts they have chosen, and they match them so perfectly with the other parts that it is astonishing' (Diodorus, I, 98). There exists in the British Museum a statue of Nefertiti which helps to corroborate this statement by Diodorus, but the invisible joints do not clearly divide up the different parts of the body (Griffith, *J.E.A.*, 1928, p. 34).

[17] D. E. Derry, *Note on the skeleton hitherto believed to be that of King Akhenaton, A.S.A.*, XXXI, p. 115.

[18] E. Meyer, *Geschichte ders Altertume* (Berlin) 1928, II, p. 34. See also C. U. A. Kappers, *An Introduction to the Anthropology of the Near East* (Chap. VI, 'The migration of the Caspian Indo-Aryans', Amsterdam, 1934).

## CHAPTER V

[1] E. Cavaignac, *Subbiluliuma et son temps* (Strasbourg) 1932, p. 50.

[2] Pendlebury, *op. cit.* p. 146.

[3] Davies, *op. cit.* III, tomb of Huya, no. 1.

[4] This state of things is described on the great stele at Karnak, consecrated by Tutankhamen at the time of the Amunian restoration at Thebes but it is probable that it existed ever since the departure of the Court for Amarna (G. Legrain, *Recueil*, 29, 1907, p. L62 ff.; English translation by Bennett in *J.E.A.*, XXV, p. 8–15).

[5] See Chapter IV, note 13.

[6] Elliot Smith, *op. cit.* p. 55. Also Derry in *A.S.A.*, 1931, XXXI, p. 115.

[7] On this controversial question see Chapter II, note 11; also R. Engelbach, 'The so-called coffin of Akhenaton', in *A.S.A.*, 1931, XXXI, p. 98–114. Also Sir Alan Gardiner, 'The so-called Tomb of Queen Tiyi'. *J.E.A.* 1957, XLIII, pp. 10–25, and G. Roeder, 'Thronfolger und Künig Smenchka-re', *Z.A.S.* 83, 1958, pp. 43–74, where the author summarizes the question and groups the monuments representing Smenkhkere, found in Memphis, Amarna and Hermopolis.

[8] N. de G. Davies, 'Akhenaten at Thebes', *J.E.A.*, IX, pp. 132–52.

[9] This is an hypothesis of my own. There exists a curious mummy in the Cairo Museum (Elliot-Smith, *op. cit.* no. 61052). It is the 'Royal daughter, royal sister' Meritamun. Smith describes her as a little old woman, twisted and dried up, probably dating from the end of the XVIIIth dynasty (use of resin under the skin as in the mummy of Amenophis III). The skull has a cephalic index smaller than that of Tutankhamen and Smenkhkere; but it is big and ovoid, the face is oval with pointed chin and spoilt teeth. She seems to have died consequently to a stroke or having been poisoned. Could she be the widow of Smenkhkere? The fact that she is not indicated as Queen would be because the 'heretic Kings' had been effaced from all the monuments at the time of Horemheb's restoration.

[10] H. Brummer, 'Eine neue Amarna Prinzessin', *Z.A.S.*, 74, 1938, p. 104. On a stone block, found at Hermopolis by the German excavators, we read the inscription: 'The own beloved royal daughter Anchesen-paten, born from the own royal daughter Anchesenpaten. . . . Nefer-kheperu-re (Uanenre = Akhenaten), who gave her life. . . .'

[11] C. E. Wilbour, *Travels in Egypt* (Brooklyn) 1936, p. 558. The author relates that he was asked, in 1890, at Amarna, to buy Akhenaten's Heart-scarab, wrapped in a sheet of gold. Now, as this was always placed on the mummy, it implied that the body had been buried in the tomb made for it, and which had been ransacked in the course of time.

[12] Legrain, *op. cit.* and above note 5.

[13] Tutankhamen and Ay continue the decoration of the Temple of Aten in Karnak. Cf. Maspero, *Histoire* . . . II, p. 335, note 2 and pp. 345 and also M. Doresse, *op. cit.*

[14] Davies and Gardiner, *The Tomb of Huy* (E.E.S., London) 1926.

[15] In 1933 appeared the three volumes of *The Tomb of Tut Ankh Amen* by H. Carter, London, 1923, 1933 and since then, Christiane Desroches-Noblecourt, *Vie et Mort d'un pharaon, Toutankhamon* (Paris, Hachette) 1963.

[16] A. H. Sayce, 'Hittite Letters on Egypt', *A.E.* 1922, III. See also W. Wolf, 'Semenchkere und Tutan-chamun', *Z.A.S.*, 65, 1930, p. 101. In 1940, Engelbach, *A.S.A.* XL, p. 141, was of the opinion that the author of the letter was actually Tutankhamen's widow. For another version of the letter, see Edel, *J.N.E.S.* 1948, VII, p. 14.

[17] P. Newberry, 'King Ay, the successor of Tutankhamun', *J.E.A.*, XVIII, 1932, p. 50, who speaks of a ring in glass with the united names of Ankhsenamun and Ay.

[18] See above note 15.

[19] *A.R.* III, 1ff.

[20] Pendlebury, *op. cit.* p. 169.

# EPILOGUE

[1] *A.R.* III, 45ff. See also Pflüger, *J.N.E.S.*, 1946, p. 160ff.

[2] H. Frankfort, *Ancient Egyptian Religion* (New York, Columbia University Press), p. 25.

[3] Davies, *The rock Tombs* . . . VI, tomb of Ay.

[4] J. H. Breasted, *A History of Egypt*, New York, 1905, p. 371. By the same, *The Dawn of Conscience* (New York, 1935) p. 367 ff.

[5] G. Nagel, 'A propos des rapports du Psaume 104 avec les textes égyptiens', *Festschrift Alfred Bertholet zum 80 Geburtstage* (Tubingen) 1950, pp. 395–403, where the author considers one should discount a direct and necessary comparison between the 104th Psalm and Aton's hymn. Could there have been a Phoenician intermediary?

[6] There were discovered at Amarna two fragments of the Epics of Erekigal and of Nergal (see *The Tell el Amarna Tablets*, no. 357, 356, 359.

[7] P. Gilbert, *op. cit.* p. 33ff.

[8] R. Berthelot, *op. cit.* p. 226

[9] With reference to the linguistical diffusions see R. Schwab, 'Domaine Oriental', in *Encyclopédie des Littératures* (Paris, La Pléiade) 1956, p. 122. He cites Filliozat who suggests possible affinities between Indo-Iranians, Akkadians, Hittites and Mitannians. He adds (p. 336) that 'the syncretisms create in the course of time a general phrasology applicable in every circumstance, without regard to the divine personality'.

[10] H. Oldenberg, *La Religion des Védas* (Paris, Alcan) 1903, p. 27.

[11] H. de Willman-Grabowska, *L'Inde antique* (Paris, Evolution de l'Humanité) p. 270.

[12] Masson-Oursel, *l'Inde antique (idem*, p. 17). Let us add further that among the Amarna Letters, two were written in Mitannian (Kanisian), a language clearly Indo-European whose forms, particularly in the names of the divinities, are very similar to those in 'Sanskrit' (*Encycl. Brit.* XII, p. 266; O. R. Gurney, *The Hittites*, 1952, ch. vi, with bibliography). It is well to remember that the Vedic divinities are mentioned in an Anatolian document of XIVth century B.C., the treaty called 'of Mitanni' where a vocabulary similar to Sanskrit is to be found.

# PLATES IN COLOUR

I. *Amenophis III in youth*. Black basalt; 60 cm. Beginning of his reign. Provenance unknown. Brooklyn Museum (N.Y.), inventory no. 59.19. This head from a colossal statue dates from early in the reign. We recognize already the full almond-eyed face which reappears in the later portraits of the sovereign. (Ekatachrome: Courtesy of Brooklyn Museum.)

II. *Statuette of Amenophis III*. Ebony overlaid with gilded stucco; eyes incrusted with opaque glass; 26 cm. Probably from Thebes. Mid-reign of Amenhotep III. Broklyn Museum (N.Y.), inventory no. 48.28.

Already the work is marked by a certain naturalism which does not hesitate to stress the king's corpulence. (Ektachrome: Courtesy of Brooklyn Museum.)

III. *Head of Queen Tiy*. Ebony overlaid with stucco and gilded linen. Found in the ruins of a palace in the Fayum. Middle or end of reign of Amenophis III. Berlin, Staatliche Museen, inventory no. 21.834.

Thanks to a head bearing the queen's name, found at Sinai (Cairo no. 38.257), we recognize the short face and sulky mouth of the sovereign: but here, marked by age. (Ektachrome: Courtesy of Aegyptische Abteilung, Staatlichen Museen, Berlin.)

IV. *Stele of Amenophis III and Tiy*. Painted limestone; 30 cm. From Amarna. End of reign of Amenophis III. British Museum, inventory no. 57.399.

Though this stele was found in an Amarna house, it was most likely made at Thebes, at the time of the third royal Jubilee, and brought to Amarna by its owner. (Ektachrome, A. Mekhitarian: Courtesy of the British Museum Trustees.)

V. *Engraved Stone from a Bracelet*. Cornelian (the gold setting is modern); 5 cm. From Thebes. End of Amenophis III's reign; Metropolitan Museum, N.Y., inventory no. 26.7.1339.

The scene represents the Pharaoh's Jubilee; the king and queen are seated side by side, with two of their daughters paying them homage. (Ektachrome: Courtesy of Metropolitan Museum of Art, N.Y.)

VI. *Flower-shaped Necklace*. Faience. From Amarna; British Museum. (Ektachrome, A. Mekhitarian; Courtesy of British Museum Trustees.)

VII. *Multi-coloured Vase*; 8 cm. From Amarna. Brussels, Musées Royaux d'Art et d'Historie, inventory no. E. 6354. (Ektachrome, A. Mekhitarian.)

VIII. *Flask in Fish-form*. Multicoloured glass; L2.5 cm. From Amarna. British Museum, inventory no. 55.193.

IX. *The Princesses at their Parent's feet*. Painting on plaster; about 35 by 30 cm. From the king's bedroom, Amarna. Ashmolean Museum, inventory no. 1893.1.

This fragment is all that remains of a large mural painting that showed the entire royal family in the familiar attitudes we find in the small private shrines. (Ektachrome: Courtesy of Skira, Geneva.)

X. *Bust of Nefertiti*. Polychrome limestone; 50 cm. From the Studio of Tuthmosis, Amarna; mid-reign of Akhenaten. Ostberliner Museum, inventory 21.300.

This bust was not a portrait in the sense we give that term today, but simply a model, an ideal model to which the definitive work was to conform. Thus the left socket was left deliberately empty, for reasons of technical training. (Ektachrome: M. Hirmer, München.)

XI. *The same, in profile.*

XII. *Painted Pavement.* Painting on plaster; 10.40 m. by 4.68 m. From the Official Palace, Amarna. Cairo Museum, inventory no. G. 627. (Ektachrome: H. Hirmer, München.)

XIII. *Fragment of a Head of Queen Tiy(?).* Yellow jasper; 13 cm. Probably from Amarna. Metropolitan Museum, N.Y., inventory no. 26.7. 1396.

This admirable fragment is all that remains of a composite statue in which the face, hands and feet were made of a material that suggested flesh, while the body was in limestone representing a pleated robe. Yellow was the conventional colour for women, while red was reserved for male figures. We recognize Tiy's expressive mouth.

(Ektachrome: Courtesy of Metropolitan Museum of Art, N.Y.)

XIV. *Head of a Princess (Ankesenpaaten?).* Reddish silicious sandstone; 29 cm. From the Studio of Tuth-mosis, Amarna. Cairo Museum, inventory no. 44.869.

One of the many heads of princesses with distorted skulls, with a tenon at the base of the throat serving to fix it in body made of some other material. C. Aldred (*New Kingdom Art in Ancient Egypt*, London, 1961) suggests that we see in it the Wife of Tutankhamen, because of its likeness to the face of the goddesses of the Pharaoh's sarcophagus. (Ektachrome: A. Mekhitarian.)

XV. *Profile of Smenkhkere.* Polychrome sandstone; 30 cm. From the official Palace, Amarna. Brooklyn Museum, N.Y. (Ektachrome: Courtesy of Brooklyn Museum.)

XVI. *Smenkhkere and Meritaten.* Painted limestone; 20 by 25 cm. From Memphis (?); Staatliche Museen, Berlin, inventory no. 15.000. This charming genre-scene dates from the short co-regency of Akhenaten and Smenkhkere, at the time when the latter set out for Memphis and Thebes to attempt a reconciliation with the Amunian opposition. (Ektachrome: Courtesy of Aegyptische Abteilung, Staatliche Museen, Berlin.)

XVII. *Canopic Head of Smenkhkere.* Alabaster, with incrusted eyes; 36 cm. From Thebes. Cairo Museum, inventory no. G. 3610.

Three Heads of Canopic Jars in alabaster were found in the tomb of Tiy with the mummy of Smenkhkere. As Maspero has remarked (*Guide du Musée du Caire* p. 370), the profile strongly suggests that of the statue from the Salt Collection in the Louvre, which very probably was this Pharaoh's. (Ektachrome: A. Mekhitarian.)

XVIII. *Head of a Ushabti of Akhenaten.* Crystalline limestone; 5 by 5 cm. From Amarna (?) Musées Royaux d'Art et d'Histoire, Brussels, inventory no. E. 6845. (Ektachrome: A. Mekhitarian.)

XIX. *Statuette of a King (Tutankhaten?).* Painted limestone; 7 cm. From Amarna. Musées Royaux d'Art et d'Histoire, Brussels, inventory no. E. 6730. (Ektachrome: A. Mekhitarian.)

XX. *Tutankhamen and Ankhesenamun.* Casket-cover; wood covered with ivory plaques; 31 cm. From Tutankhamun's tomb at Thebes. Cairo Museum, inventory no. 1189. (Ektachrome: M. Hirmer.)

XXI. *Negro tributaries arriving at Thebes.* Painting on Plaster. From tomb of the Viceroy of Kush, Huy (Tomb no. 40) at Thebes; reign of Tutankhamun. (Ektachrome: Skira, Geneva.)

XXII. *Tutankhamun in his war-chariot fighting Syrians.* Casket from his tomb. Cairo Museum, Tutankhamun Collection, inventory no. 324. (Photograph, M. Hirmer.)

XIII. *Head of Amun.* Mauve quartzite; 18 cm. Found at Karnak. Cairo Museum, inventory no. J. 38.002. Reign of Tutankhamun.

It belongs without doubt to a statuette restored by Tutankhamun and thus bears the Pharaoh's features. (Ektachrome: A. Mekhitarian.)

XXIV. *Statuette of a Gazelle.* Ivory; 15 cm. From Thebes; reign of Tutankhamun (?) Metropolitan Museum, N.Y., inventory no. 26.7. 1292. (Ektachrome: Courtesy of Metropolitan Museum.)

# MONOCHROME ILLUSTRATIONS

1. *Detail from the frame of Tuthmosis IV's chariot.* Linen and gilded stucco on a wooden frame; 32 by 42 cm. From the king's tomb at Thebes, XVIIIth dynasty. Cairo Museum, inv. no. 46.097.

2. *Counting cattle.* Limestone. Tomb of Khaemhat (no. 57) at Thebes; under Amenophis III. (Courtesy: Metropolitan Museum of Art, N.Y.)

3. *Amenophis III on his throne.* Limestone, same tomb as previous item. (Courtesy: Metropolitan Museum of Art, N.Y.)

4. *Queen Tiy.* Limestone; 42 cm. From the tomb of Userhat (no. 47) at Thebes. Musées Royaux d'Art et d'Histoire, Brussels, inv. no. E. 2157. (Photo: A.C.L., Brussels.)

5. *Stele of a Syrian Soldier.* Painted Limestone. From Amarna. Staatliche Museen, Berlin, inv. no. 14.122.

6. *The Palace of Amenophis III at Malkata.* View towards the south. Thebes, the left bank of the Nile. (Courtesy of Metropolitan Museum of Art, N.Y.)

7. *Detail of the pillared hall of Amun's Temple, Luxor.* View from the south-west. XVIIIth dynasty.

8. *Amenophis III's Bedroom, towards the north-west, Palace of Malkata.* Thebes, left bank, XVIIIth dynasty. (Courtesy of Metropolitan Museum of Art, N.Y.)

9. *View of Birket Habu,* the ancient pleasure-lake of Queen Tiy. Malkata, Thebes, left bank, XVIIIth dynasty. (Courtesy of Metropolitan Museum of Art, N.Y.)

10. *Banquet Scene.* Tomb of Deserkarasonb (no. 38). Thebes, Tuthmosis IV. (Courtesy of Metropolitan Museum of Art, N.Y.)

11. *Armchair of Satamun.* Wood; 77 by 52 by 54 cm. Tomb of Yuia and Tuiu, Thebes, Amenhotep III. Cairo Museum, inv. no. 51.113.

12. *Letter of Amenophis III to Milkili, King of Gezer.* Baked clay; 7 by 5.2 cm. From Amarna (?). Musées Royaux d'Art et d'Histoire, Brussels, inv. no. E. 6753. (Photo: A.C.L., Brussels.)

13. *Headless Statue of Amenophis III.* Black serpentine; 22 cm. From Thebes (?). Metropolitan Museum of Art, N.Y., inv. no. 30.8.74. (Courtesy of Metropolitan Museum of Art, N.Y.)

14. *Amenophis IV (Akhenaten) and Nefertiti, followed by Meritaten, officiating before Aten's altar.* Limestone; 80 cm. Fragment of a balustrade from the official Palace, Amarna. Cairo Museum, inv. no. 20.11.26.4.

15. *Fragment of a colossus of Amenophis IV.* Sandstone. From the temple of Aten, Karnak. Inv. no. N/E. XIII.

16. *Osirian Statue of Amenophis IV.* Polychrome sandstone; 310 cm. From the temple of Aten at Karnak. Cairo Museum, inv. no. 49.528.

17. *Detail of previous item.*

18. *The brother of Ramose and his wife.* Limestone; about 140 cm. From Ramose's tomb (no. 55) at Thebes; start of reign of Amenophis IV. (Courtesy of the Metropolitan Museum of Art, N.Y.)

19. *Ramose receiving the homage of foreign envoys.* After the sketch by M. Baud. Tomb of Ramose (no. 55) at Thebes. Start of Amenophis IV's reign.

20. *Akhenaten sacrificing before the altar of Aten.* Limestone; 24.5 by 54.5 cm. From Amarna. A.R.A.C.,

no. 9. Norbert Schimmel Collection, New York, no. 105. This extraordinary scene in which the Pharaoh prepares to wring the neck of a duck before the god, is unique of its kind. (Photo: O. E. Nelson, N.Y.)

21. *Aerial View of el-Amarna.* The central quarter, towards the north. In the foreground, the storehouses and dwellings of the priests attached to the great Temple; then the little Temple, the royal domain. On the left of the latter, we see the ruins of the bridge linking it to the official Palace, which stretches out on the left and disappears under cultivated ground. At the back, the great Temple, which had not yet been excavated at the time when the photo was taken. (Photo: R.A.F.)

22. *Landscape of el-Amarna.* The north cliff, overhanging the Nile. (Photo: A. Mekhitarian.)

23. *Boundary Stele, South Amarna.* (Photo: A. Mekhitarian.)

24. *Ruins of the northern Palace, Amarna.* (Photo: A. Mekhitarian.)

25. *Department of Archives, Amarna,* situated on the east of the royal domain. Here were found the largest number of baked clay tablets.

26. *Aerial View of el-Amarna.* The northern district, seen from the west. (Photo: R.A.F.)

27. *Reconstruction of the central quarter, Amarna.* (After *The City of Akhenaten,* III, pl. ii.)

28. *Ladies of Honour in a chariot,* following the royal procession. Limestone; 23.5 by 54.7 cm. From Amarna. A.R.A.C. no. 33. Norbert Schimmel Collection, N.Y., no. 120. (Photo: J. D. Schiff, N.Y.)

29. *Reconstruction of the Great Temple, Amarna.* (After *The City of Akhenaten,* III, pl. ix.)

30. *Ruins of the House of General Ramose; Amarna.* (Photo: A. Mekhitarian.)

31. *Foreign Musicians, with bandaged eyes.* Limestone; 22 by 24.5 cm. From Amarna; A.R.A.C. no. 45. Norbert Schimmel Collection, N.Y., no. 124. (Photo: O. E. Nelson, N.Y.)

32. *The Preparations of the Royal Boat.* Limestone; 23.3 by 54.3 cm. From Amarna; A.R.A.C., no. 50. Norbert Schimmel Collection, N.Y., no. 119. The boat is moored at the foot of the great Palace. On the right is seen a part of the royal garden. On the kiosk, on the boat's stern, is a representation of the king laying an enemy low, with the queen nearby. (Photo: O. E. Nelson, N.Y.)

33. *Horses in Harness.* Limestone; 23 by 52 cm. From Amarna; A.R.A.C., no. 33. Norbert Schimmel, N.Y. (Photo: O. E. Nelson, N.Y.)

34. *The Princess eating a Chicken.* Ostracon on limestone, used for a sculptural maquette. Found in the court of the great Temple, Amarna. Cairo Museum. There is a subtle variety in the different planes of the relief, which attains a great delicacy in the finished parts.

35. *Courtiers with Fan-holders and Ladies of Honour.* Limestone; 23 by 54 cm. From Amarna; A.R.A.C., no. 19. Norbert Schimmel Collection, N.Y., no. 114. (Photo: O. E. Nelson, N.Y.)

36. *Funerary Ceremonies of Makitaten.* Lamentations before the cenotaph. After the drawing by M. Baud. Limestone. From the royal tomb at Amarna.

37. *Courtiers playing Homage to the Royal Couple.* Limestone; 22.5 by 54 cm. From Amarna; A.R.A.C., no. 14. Norbert Schimmel Collection, N.Y., no. 111.

38. *The king making an offering.* Limestone; 21 by 34.5 cm. From Hermopolis (Amarna?); A.R.A.C., no. 7. Norbert Schimmel Collection, N.Y., no. 106. See G. Roeder, *M.D.I. für Agyptische Altertumskunde in Kairo* 9, 1940, p. 17. (Photo: O. E. Nelson, N.Y.)

39. *Ladies of the court at an official ceremony.* Limestone; 21.5 by 53.5 cm. From Amarna; A.R.A.C., no. 23. Norbert Schimmel Collection, N.Y., no. 118. Attempts have been made to identify the curious instrument that the women lift to their mouth like cups. Are they not rather small musical instruments (of the ocarina kind)? (Photo: O.E. Nelson, N.Y.)

40. *The King's Hand.* Limestone; 21 by 34.5 cm. From Amarna, A.R.A.C., no. 2. Norbert Schimmel Collection, N.Y., no. 104. Akhenaten has just let fall the offering of fat on to the god's altar. (Photo: D. Widmer, Basle.)

41. *Painted Pavement, Duck and Plants.* Painting on plaster. From Amarna. Metropolitan Museum, N.Y., inv. no. 20.2.2. (Photo: Courtesy of Metropolitan Museum of Art, N.Y.)

42 *A Bunch of Grapes.* Limestone; 23 by 42 cm. From Amarna; A.R.A.C., no. 59. Norbert Schimmel Collection, N.Y., no. 127. (Photo: O E. Nelson, N.Y.)

43. *A Field of Corn.* Limestone; 23 by 52 cm. From Amarna, A.R.A.C., no. 57. Norbert Schimmel Collection, N.Y., no. 128. (Photo: O. E. Nelson, N.Y.)

44. *Two Profiles of Akhenaten.* Sculptors' Draughts. A. Limestone; 26 cm. Found in the great Temple, Amarna. Brooklyn Museum. The ink sketch has begun to be cut out by the chisel; the profile has been detached. (Attempts have been made to see Nefertiti in it; but we recognize the jaw-structure characteristic of Akhenaten, Tiy, and Ay.) B. Caricatural relief. Limestone; 15 cm. From Amarna. Staatliche Museen, Berlin, inv. no. 14.512

45. *Small Stele representing Akhenaten and his Family.* Limestone. From Amarna. Staatliche Museen, Berlin, inv. no. 14.145.

46. *Two fragments of private stelae.* A. Limestone. From Amarna. Staatliche Museen, Berlin, inv. no. 14.511. B. Limestone. From Amatna. Louvre Museum, Paris, inv, no. ii. 624.

47. *Mask of Ay( ?).* Plaster; 24 cm. Studio of Tuthmosis, Amarna. Staatliche Museen, Berlin, inv. no. 21.350. The attribution is supported by comparing the mask's features, on the one side with the colossus of Ay in the Berlin Museum (no. 1479), and on the other with an anonymous head in the Cairo Museum (No. N.E. vii) which seems certainly the head of Ay: see J. Vandier, Manuel, t. III, Paris, 1958. pp. 368, x 371). Despite the marked stylization which almost turns the mask into a model (the striations on the eyelids are the same as on the polychrome bust of Nefertiti), the highly naturalistic anatomy of the sterno-mastoidian muscle, visible when the head is thrown back, shows clearly that the mask has been moulded from life.

48. *The sane mask im profile.*

49. *Head of Tiy.* See plate III. The close resemblance of this profile and that of the mask gives strong support to the very tempting and plausible hypothesis of C. Aldred, that the two persons were brother and sister.

50. *Mask of Neferiti in profile.* Brown sandstone; 30.2 cm. From Tuthmosis' studio in Amarna. Staatliche Museen, Berlin, inv. no. 21, 220. Very like the polychrome bust of the queen this head seems to have been directly inspired by it.

51. *Mask of Nefertiti in profile.* Plaster; 25 cm. From Tuthmosis' studio in Amarna. Staatliche Museen, Berlin, inv. no. 21.349. It is interesting to compare the profiles of this and the previous item; the resemblance is striking and helps to confirm the attribution of the queen.

52. *Mask of Akhenaten, in profile.* Plaster; 29.7 cm. From Tuthmosis' studio in Amarna. Staatliche Museen, Berlin, inv. no. 21.348.

53. *Model of Akhenaten, in profile.* Plaster; 26 cm. From Tuthmosis' Studio in Amarna. Staatliche Museen, Berlin, inv. no. 21.351.

54. *Mask of Akhenaten, full face.* The mask has been moulded directly on the king's face. It is then the most veracious portrait of him, and also the most 'spiritual' of all those that we know. We can compare it with the bust in the Louvre (see no. 84 here).

55. *Plaster-cast of Akhenaten, full face.* Is this a study of the sovereign or a mould made after a work of sculpture, to preserve its model?

56. *Deathmask of the Princess Makitaten( ?).* Plaster; 20.4 cm. From Tuthmosis' Studio in Amarna. Staatliche Museen, Berlin, inv, 21.340.

57. *Head of the Princess Makitaten ( ?).* Brown sandstone; ii cm. From Tuthmosis' Studio in Amarna. Staatliche Museen, Berlin, inv. no. 21. 245. Thanks to a tiny fragment of an washabti (now in the Brooklyn Museum), which, according to the hypothesis of J. Capart, belonged to the Princess Makitaten, we have been able to relate it to this head as well as the previous mask.

58. *Model of Amenophis III.* Plaster; 22 cm. From Tuthmosis' Studio in Amarna. Staatliche Museen, Berlin, inv. no. 21.299. This model has been probably moulded on a sculptured work. Vandier (op. *cit.*) relates it convincingly to the face of the Brooklyn statue (pl. II here), which certainly represents Amenophis III.

59. *Deathmask of Amenophis III( ?).* Plaster; 18 cm. From Tuthmosis' Studio in Amarna. Staatliche Museen, Berlin, inv. no. 21.356. This attribution by Schäfer is confirmed by the presence of the king's model and also by certain details: the mouth sunken in through the absence of incisors and the suffering expression. The eyes are only half-open, proving that the mask has been moulded on the face.

60. *Model of Amenophis III in profile.*

61. *Deathmask of Amenophis III ( ?) in profile.*

62. *Mask of Nefertiti ( ?),* Plaster; 25 cm. From Tuthmosis' Studio in Amarna. Staatliche Museen, Berlin, inv. no. 21.349. This mask has been moulded on a living model; the eyes have been opened up afterwards on the closed eyelids. It is of interest to compare this mask with that of Cairo, found in Amarna in 1932, which shows the queen's face emaciated and aged.

63. *Statuette of Queen Nefertiti( ?).* Limestone; 41 cm. From Tuthmosis' Studio in Amarna. Staatliche Museen, Berlin, inv. no. 21.263. Broken at the ankles and the right arm, and restored in antiquity. Without being a portrait, this statuette certainly represents the queen, her body grown heavy through her many childbirths. She is not nude as some have asserted, but is clad in a transparent robe that lets the detail of her body show through.

64. *Profile of Smenkhkere.* Inset for a relief, Reddish Sandstone; 12 cm. From the Great Temple, Amarna. Brooklyn Museum.

65. *Unfinished head of Nefertiti.* Grey granite; 23 cm. From Tuthmosis' Studio in Amarna. Staatliche Museen, Berlin, inv. no. 21. 358.

66. *Study for a Bust of Nefertiti.* Limestone; 28.7 cm. From Tuthmosis' Studio in Amarna. Staatliche Museen, Berlin, inv. no. 21.352. This head is taken usually as a preparatory study for the polychrome bust; but a careful comparison of the two faces makes us believe rather the contrary—that it is a study after the bust, a mediocre study which the master's hand has corrected in black ink.

67. *Unfinished head of Nefertiti.* Rose Quartzite; 33 cm. From Amarna. Cairo Museum, inv. no. 59. 286.

68. *Head of a Princess (Meritaten?).* Brown sandstone; 21.2 cm. From Tuthmosis' Studio in Amarna. Staatliche Museen, Berlin, inv. no. 21.223.

69. *Head of Princess.* Painted limestone; 14 cm. From Amarna. Staatliche Museen, Berlin, inv. no. 14.113.

70. *Deathmask of an Unknown Man.* Plaster; 24; cm. From Tuthmosis' Studio in Amarna. Staatliche Museen, Berlin, inv. no. 21.228. Borchardt considered it as one of the rare examples moulded from nature, in which the eyes were afterwardes opened. It seems rather that the subject was moulded with open eyes, as is suggested by the trace of an air-bubble caught in the mould on the left eye, as well as the bulge on the upper part of the eyelids.

71. *Bust of Princess Makitaten (?).* Painted limestone; 22.5 cm. From Amarna (?). Louvre Museum, Paris, inv. no. E. 14.715. The princess wears a wig with the lock of hair belonging to royal children as well as the pleated robe and the large pectoral (compare the relief, no. 75 here). The face is very close to the portraits we believe to be Makitaten's

72. *Head of Princess Makitaten (?).* See mo. 57 here.

73. *Deathmask of Princess Makitaten (?).* See mo. 56 here.

74. *Female musicans.* Limestone; 21 by 53 cm. From Amarna; A.R.A.C., no. 42. Norbert Schimmel Collection, N.Y., no. 116. From left to right: a harp-player, two lute-players, a singer, and a lyre- player. (Photo: O. E. Nelson, N.Y.)

75. *Two Princesses.* Limsetone; 22 by 28 cm. From Hermopolis (Amarna ?): see G. Roeder, *Ein Jahrzehnt Deutscher Ausgrabungen in Agypytn*, 1951, pl. 14(b); A.R.A.C., no. 16. The princess is represented with her torso to the front, a very rare instance, unknown before the Amarna period. (Photo: O. E. Nelson, N.Y.)

76. *Female dancers and singers.* Limestone; 24 by 37.2 cm. From Amarna; A.R.A.C., no. 44. Norbert Schimmel Collection, N.Y., no. 115. (Photo: O. E. Nelson, N.Y.)

77. *Head of Smenkhkere (?).* Brownish-yellow quartzite; 17.8 cm. From Memphis. Cairo Museum, inv. no. J. 45. 547. As C. Aldred (*New Kingdom Art in Ancient Egypt*, London, 1961, no. 135) suggests, this head lacks the features of either Akhenaten or Tutankhamen, and so may be taken as representing Smenkhkere and dating from his co-regency, at the time of his journey to Menmphis.

78. *Princess Ankhesenpaaten making an offering of loaves to Aten.* Limestone; 22.2 by 54 cm. From Amarna; A.R.A.C., no. 10. Norbert Schimmel Collection, N.Y., no. 109. (Photo: O. E. Nelson, N.Y.)

79. *Sculptor's Model of Smenkhkeare (?).* Painted limestone; 21 cm. From Amarna. Staatliche Museen, Berlin, inv. no. 20. 469. This model did not come from Tuthmosis's studio; it came from another and shows that the way of working was not very different in other studios. We do not know any certain portraits of Smenkhkere; it is only by deduction that we identify them. Here is a royal head, which certainly does not represent Akhenaten or Tutankhamen. C. Aldred correctly links if with the statue from the Salt Collection in the Louvre (see no. 83 here.)

80. *Relief-Model of Smenkhkere (?).* Limestone. From Amarna. Staatliche Museen, Berlin, inv. no.21. 683.

81. *Stele representing Akhenaten and Smenkhkere.* Limestone. From Amarna. Staatliche Museen, Berlin, inv. no. 17.813.

82. *Unfinished Stele of Akhenaten and Smenkhkere.* Limestone. From Amarna. Staatliche Museen, Berlin, inv. no. 20. 716.

83. *Seated Statue of Smenkhkere (?).* Yellow steatite; 61 cm. From Thebes (?). Louvre Museum, Paris, inv. no. N. 831 (previously in the Salt Collection). Uninscribed statue which once formed part of a group. Aldred proposes to see Smenkhkere in it; and his arguments seem to us firmly based. It is certanly, by its style, a work of the close of the Amarna period, which is related to sculptures of the Theban restoration. (See Vandier, *op. cit.*, who goes into all the arguments, pp. 345–47.)

84. *Bust of Akhenaten.* Limestone; 55 cm. From Amarna (?). Louvre Museum, Paris inv. no. E. 11076. Although its surface is corroded by saltpetre, this bust remains, in J. Vandier's phrase (*op. cit.* p. 339), 'the master piece of the school.' Like its fellow of Berlin (no. 21. 360), which was found broken in Tuthmosis' studio, it must have served as a studio-model.

85. *Unfinished group of Akhenaten and a Princess.* Limestone; 40 cm. From Tuthmosis' Studio in Amarna.

Cairo Museum, inv. no. 44. 866. We have here, transposed into the round, a familiar subject on the private stelae.

86. *Asian Prisoners*. Limestone; 16 cm. From the tomb of General Horemheb, Memphis. Leyden Museum, inv. no. 45. At the time he commanded the Pharaoh's armies and resided at Memphis, Horemheb had a tomb prepared for himself, which he never occupied. He sets out in it his military exploits in Palestine. The tomb was dismembered early in the XIXth century and brought back to Europe by Belzoni. Fragments are found in many museums (Bologna, Leyden, Louvre, and Brooklyn).

87. *Negro Prisoners*, Limestone; 30 cm. From the tomb of General Horemheb, Memphis. Civic Museum, Bologna, inv. no. 1889.

88. *The Nubian Princess and her Attendants*. Painting on plaster. From the tomb of the Viceray of Nubia, Huy (no. 40), Thebes. Period of Tutankhamen.

89. *Horseman*. Limestone; 16 cm. From the tomb of Horemheb, Memphis. Civic Museum, Bologna, inv. no. 1889.

90. *Ay as the Nile God*. Crystalline limestone; 45 cm. From Medinet-Habu. Boston Museum, inv. no. 50. 3789. The face shows Ay's features idealised and rendered impersonal. Ay became Pharaoh on Tutankhamen's death. This fragment belonged to one of the sides of the throne of a seated colossus, which must have adorned the funerary temple of the king. (Photo: Courtesy of the Museum of Fine Arts, Boston.)

91. *Statue of General Horemheb as Scribe*. Grey granite; 110 cm. From Memphis. Metropolitan Museum of Fine Arts, N.Y., inv. no. 23. 101

92. *Detail of a Procession* (?). Limestone; 24.1 by 53.5 cm; A.R.A.C., no. 21. Norbert Schimmel Collection, N.Y. The persons are clearly foreigners, but it is hard to make out what they are doing. (Photo: D. Widmer, Basle.)

93. *The King making an Offering*. Limestome; 22 by 44 cm.; A.R.A.C., no. 1. Norbert Schimmel Collection, N.Y. no. 107.

94. *Mazoi Troops of the Royal Escort*. Limestone; 21.6 by 46.7 cm.; A.R.A.C., no. 22. Norbert Schimmel Collection N.Y., (Photo: O. E. Nelson, N.Y.)

95. *Asian Head*. Yellow limestone; 6.1 cm.; end of the XVIIIth dynasty. Norbert Schimmel Collection, N.Y., no. 91.

96. *Lid of a Pot for Costmetics*. Wood; 10.3 cm. in diameter. End of XVIIIth dynasty. Norbert Schimmel Collection N.Y., no. 92. (Photo: O. E. Nelson, N. Y.)

Illustrations without reference to a photographer come from the Archives of the Fondation Egyptologique Reine Elizabeth at Brussels.